Reading Motivation

Reading Motivation

A Guide to Understanding and Supporting Children's Willingness to Read

Joy Dangora Erickson

ROWMAN & LITTLEFIELD
Lanham • Boulder • New York • London

Published by Rowman & Littlefield
An imprint of The Rowman & Littlefield Publishing Group, Inc.
4501 Forbes Boulevard, Suite 200, Lanham, Maryland 20706
www.rowman.com

86-90 Paul Street, London EC2A 4NE, United Kingdom

Copyright © 2023 by Joy Dangora Erickson

All rights reserved. No part of this book may be reproduced in any form or by any electronic or mechanical means, including information storage and retrieval systems, without written permission from the publisher, except by a reviewer who may quote passages in a review.

British Library Cataloguing in Publication Information Available

Library of Congress Cataloging-in-Publication Data

Names: Erickson, Joy Dangora, 1981– author.
Title: Reading motivation : a guide to understanding and supporting children's willingness to read / Joy Dangora Erickson.
Description: Lanham : Rowman & Littlefield, [2023] | Includes index. | Summary: "Reading Motivation supports pre-service and in-service educators in conducting systematic case studies of children's motivation to read in specific contexts. Readers are guided step-by-step through the process of conducting a case study of reading motivation from which they may better support their students' developing motivation to read"—Provided by publisher.
Identifiers: LCCN 2022035075 (print) | LCCN 2022035076 (ebook) | ISBN 9781475863499 (cloth) | ISBN 9781475863505 (paperback) | ISBN 9781475863512 (epub)
Subjects: LCSH: Reading (Elementary)—Case studies. | Motivation in education—Case studies. | Books and reading.
Classification: LCC LB1573 .E75 2023 (print) | LCC LB1573 (ebook) | DDC 372.42—dc23/eng/20220902
LC record available at https://lccn.loc.gov/2022035075
LC ebook record available at https://lccn.loc.gov/2022035076

For Gabi, who taught me how to truly listen to young children.

Contents

Foreword	ix
Preface *Joy Dangora Erickson and Luke Reynolds*	xiii
Acknowledgments	xix
Introduction	xxi
Chapter 1: Why Should I Probe My Students' Program-Specific Motivation? *Joy Dangora Erickson*	1
Chapter 2: OK, OK, I'm In! Now What?!: Defining Your Case and Refining Your Inquiry Question *Joy Dangora Erickson and Beth Fornauf*	13
Chapter 3: Standing on the Shoulders of Giants: Using the Work of Others to Support Your Project *Joy Dangora Erickson and Alessandra E. Ward*	25
Chapter 4: Data Collection: Deciding What to Collect and How to Collect It *Joy Dangora Erickson and Beth Fornauf*	39
Chapter 5: How Am I Going to Fit Data Collection into My Packed Day?: Outlining a Data Collection Plan *Joy Dangora Erickson and Kyleigh P. Rousseau*	57
Chapter 6: I Have to Analyze All of This Too?!: Drafting an Analysis Plan That Works for You *Beth Fornauf and Joy Dangora Erickson*	67

Chapter 7: Help! I'm Drowning in Data!: Making Sense of
    Qualitative Data   77
    Joy Dangora Erickson and Alessandra E. Ward

Chapter 8: What About Pre- and Post-Motivation Survey
    Scores? How Might They Support My Conclusions?: Simple
    Quantitative Data Analysis   91
    Carla M. Evans

Chapter 9: Presentations and Publications: Engaging Others in Your
    Work Inside and Outside of the Immediate Community   103
    Joy Dangora Erickson and Cara E. Furman

Chapter 10: Tweaking Your Practice, Documenting What Happens,
    and Beginning Again   115
    Joy Dangora Erickson and Alessandra E. Ward

Epilogue   127
    Joy Dangora Erickson and Cara E. Furman

Index   131

About the Author and Contributors   139

Foreword

> "What you see and what you hear depends a great deal on where you are standing. It also depends on what sort of person you are."—C. S. Lewis, *The Magician's* Nephew (1955)

This is a book about seeing—and especially about hearing—what young children have to say about their reading experiences. For many years, scholars have positioned young children (those in the primary grades, K–2) as too young, too cognitively and linguistically immature to describe their own experiences reliably. Scholars and educators have instead relied on adult observations and interpretations to represent young children's voices. This is true despite international agreement that children have the right to participate in decisions that impact their learning.

Article 12 of the United Nations Convention on the Rights of the Child (CRC) specifies that "children have the right to say what they think should happen when adults are making decisions that affect them and have their opinions taken into account" (UNICEF UK, 1989). While it remains true that the United States is the only member of the United Nations not to sign on to the treaty, Article 12 is widely agreed upon by educators, child advocates, and politicians (including at least two presidents) alike (Gradia, 2015).

The central focus of this book is on helping educators better understand young children's motivation to engage in reading programs with the goal of improving the match between a child's motivation and the practices they encounter. This book is essentially a handbook for understanding and amplifying children's voices in pursuit of more motivating—more powerful—reading instruction.

As a former elementary teacher and literacy specialist, and a rising star in the world of educational research, Joy Dangora Erickson bridges perspectives on motivation in a way few have been able to accomplish. Her deep appreciation for the ethical treatment of young children undergirds everything she does; this has been true as long as I have known her. Her experiences teaching young children enable her to view the research endeavor presented here—and it is primarily a research endeavor—through the lens of a practicing teacher.

She fully appreciates most teachers' limited experiences with formal research, the ever-increasing demands on teachers' time and attention, and teachers' deep commitment to improving the learning experiences of their students. In recognizing the realities and priorities up front, Erickson and her colleagues are able to bring teachers in on the ground level and scaffold their journey to a completed research study. Not only will educators benefit from the implementation of this model, but the field of academic motivation will benefit as well, as teachers share their findings in schools, at conferences, and in publications.

The beauty of this book is that it is as much for children as it is for teachers and scholars—indeed, throughout the book, the lines between these roles (students, teachers, scholars) are overlapping, often indistinguishable. While children will not (likely) read this book themselves, their ideas and expertise are at the heart of the model. What do individual young children value? What do they enjoy? What makes them feel successful? What is considered an imposition on their time and temperament?

The argument here is that, without understanding—really understanding—the motivations of a young child, it is not possible to create instruction that fully meets their needs. Thus, teachers must be learners. And more than casual learners, teachers are naturally in positions to act as scholars in order to learn, systematically, what motivates their students. Moreover, the authors have developed specific techniques for learning from young children: Walking interviews and narrated tours of classrooms, for example, create unique opportunities for young children to share what they know.

Whether you are a reading educator or a scholar (or both), this is a book that can be engaged in layers, as you are ready: For some, it can serve as a way to better understand motivation and motivational forces, as a way to hone your ongoing observations and questions about your students. Others will want to address those questions and observations more systematically.

For these readers, Erickson and her coauthors take you through each step of conducting a case study, from framing an argument to collecting and organizing resources, to determining what kinds of data you actually need to address your most pressing questions and sharing out your findings.

For each step, there are concrete examples and simple tools that help you keep track of what you are doing and preserve cruciall observations. The tools shared here will help you document your students' all-important voices. But the book does not stop there; the ultimate objective is not just to *document* students' viewpoints but also to *understand* those perspectives and experiences and *enact changes* that improve students' learning experiences. In keeping with Article 12 of the CRC, the goal is for young children to become full participants in their own learning experiences.

Indeed, the type of study described here has the potential to empower both educators/researchers and young children. When educators better understand their students' motivations, they are empowered to make changes. When they try out a case study approach with colleagues, they are less isolated and more connected—both in their own schools, and ultimately, within the larger community of like-minded scholars.

When young children are explicitly asked to share their views—when they recognize that their voices are being heard—they are empowered to consider their learning environments further. They take pride in their contributions and are empowered to share more. (And, of course, when teachers make changes in response to their feedback, students also engage more fully—and predictably, their reading improves.)

> "All grown-ups were children first. But only few of them remember it."—
> Antoine de Saint-Exupery, *The Little* Prince (1943)

If you have ever had the good fortune of watching Joy Dangora Erickson interact with young children, it is clear that she is one of those rare adults who remembers what it was to be a child. Perhaps it is that memory, coupled with her deep commitment to respect young children—and her personal brilliance—that led her to the methods described here. No doubt, it was enhanced by her work with her colleagues.

Whatever the exact path to the volume you now hold, this is a book that will enable you to combine inspiration and curiosity with the concrete tools needed to better understand your students' motivation. Most important, you will be able to use what you learn from your young experts to adapt and change your instructional practices in ways that improve children's experiences learning to read.

Dr. Ruth Wharton-McDonald
Associate Professor of Education
University of New Hampshire

REFERENCES

Gradia, K. (2015, December 8). *Convention on the rights of the child: The United States lags behind.* Humanium. https://www.humanium.org/en/usa-and-crc/

UNICEF UK. (1989). *The United Nations convention on the rights of the child.* https://downloads.unicef.org.uk/wp-content/uploads/2010/05/UNCRC_PRESS200910web.pdf?_ga=2.78590034.795419542.1582474737-1972578648.1582474737

Preface

Joy Dangora Erickson and Luke Reynolds

> "By utilizing the most reliable information we can gather to inform and shape our teacher research, we can justify our claims that we are constantly improving our practices so we can provide the best *experiences* possible for the children we teach."—(Hatch, 2012, p. ix; emphasis added)

Do you ever suspect that your own reading lessons or those offered by others might be eroding some students' motivation to participate in a specific reading program and/or to read more generally? Do you wonder whether certain students' reading experiences could be more joyful or meaningful? Do you ever feel that you are deadlocked in a reading program without being exactly sure what your students are really getting out of it?

Perhaps you have realized there is a substantial disconnect among the racial, social, and/or cultural representations (or lack thereof) in a reading program and students' own racial, social, and cultural identities. Maybe a specific child or group of children regularly struggles to focus, refuses to engage, or acts out during sessions. A student may even have mustered the courage to disclose personal dissatisfaction by requesting to read something else or to engage in a different activity entirely.

Though we do not claim that these more obvious manifestations of poor motivation in response to reading programs are the norm, we do maintain that when we (in our previous roles as classroom teachers and reading specialists) did find our lessons and/or reading programs to misalign with students' individual motivation profiles, we felt a strong sense of responsibility to act. We were driven to make feasible changes aimed at better supporting children's program-specific and overall reading motivation.

We did not always have the precise conceptual and theoretical language to describe what we and our students were observing, experiencing, and/or doing. However, instinctively we understood the crucial role motivation plays in supporting reading skill development and achievement, both of which undoubtedly influence and direct one's life prospects.

Think back to your own childhood. Perhaps you can recall experiencing regular frustration or being turned off by early reading lessons. Or maybe you know a close friend or sibling who had difficulty maintaining motivation for reading experiences in school. Did you or they struggle in silence; did you or they go through the motions each day to please an adult while your or their joy withered?

More students go along to get along than many realize. Across multiple case studies of K–2 students' motivation for school reading programs, the first author (Joy) identified a substantial percentage of students whom adults described as adequately engaged in their reading lessons, but who self-reported that if permitted to choose, would not attend their reading intervention for a variety of worthy reasons (Erickson, 2019; Erickson et al., 2020).

Consider the profound ramifications of this finding. Young students on the cusp of that magical world we call reading *seem* engaged, externally, in the reading lesson but, in reality, are not engaged in a deep or meaningful *internal* way. As profoundly noted by Ritchhart and colleagues (2011), we need to ask, "Are students really learning, or just learning to play the game?" (p. 221).

And furthermore, how can we proactively help young readers love to learn, internally, rather than simply learn to play the game of school, externally? Our inspiration for and commitment to writing this text largely stems from experiences discovering and working with these students, students whose low programmatic motivation might not otherwise have been identified and whom we passionately believe not only have a fundamental *right to learn how to read* but also a *right to enjoy learning how to read*.

CHRISSY'S CASE

In an effort to make the interactions with young readers that spurred us to write this text more transparent, we offer 5-year-old Chrissy's case. At the time of Joy's study (Erickson et al., 2020), Chrissy was in kindergarten and placed in a reading intervention program due to her performing below kindergarten benchmarks on a variety of reading assessments.

Chrissy attended intervention in the school's reading resource room four times per week for 25 minutes a session. Intervention sessions consisted primarily of systematic and explicit phonics instruction; however, 5 to 10 minutes per session were reserved for reading connected text.

To adults, Chrissy appeared highly engaged in her intervention sessions; the reading specialist and Joy both described Chrissy as the *most* engaged participant in her reading intervention group and in the study overall. Similarly, she scored highly on a behavioral engagement rating scale completed by adults.

However, two participatory interviews—one in which she drew what she did during intervention sessions and another in which she offered the researcher a tour of the reading intervention space—revealed that Chrissy was not nearly as big a fan of her reading intervention as the adults working with her believed. In fact, she was adamant that if *she* could decide when and where to practice her reading, it would be in her classroom with her teacher or at home with her parents.

The participatory interviews revealed Chrissy's motivational struggles in ways adult evaluations of her participation did not. Chrissy was able to describe the conditions she understood to be contributing to her not wanting to participate in the reading program.

The books provided in the program and one specific intervention tool were, according to Chrissy, primarily responsible for her low motivation for the reading intervention. Chrissy expressed that she wanted to be a park ranger when she grew up; she cared deeply for the forest's creatures and aspired to protect them one day. The adults involved in the study were blown away by the clarity and determination with which this kindergarten student spoke of her long-term goal.

Chrissy went on to explain that rarely if ever was she permitted to read books about "woodland creatures" during intervention sessions, but that her parents and classroom teacher were responsive to her interest and made efforts to help her find and read these types of books. Additionally, Chrissy took issue with some of the letter tiles she was expected to use during the systematic phonics instruction provided during intervention sessions.

Specifically, she found digraph tiles (single tiles containing two letters that make one sound) to be especially frustrating to locate when building words. Chrissy explained that she would "freeze up" when a digraph tile was required to complete an assigned word. She asked Joy to pass along to her interventionist her suggestion for being permitted to use the two individual letters that formed the digraph instead of having to remind herself to look for the additional digraph tile each time.

The articulate and insightful information offered by this young reader is impressive. The information is also valuable; small adjustments to the reading intervention can now be made in response to Chrissy's self reports.

Maximizing motivation is a top priority for us; however, motivation ought to be a top priority for everyone concerned with furthering children's reading proficiency. Imagine what might happen if we spent more time striving to better understand children's own perceptions of their reading experiences and less time assuming that we know what is best for them.

Chrissy's compliance in her intervention program was clearly mistaken for high motivation and engagement, and the changes she suggested be made to improve her experience are certainly not extreme. Simply seeking out or creating short passages of connected text rooted in her interests could be all that is needed to boost her motivation for the intervention and better support her developing reading proficiency. We maintain that learning more about children's individual experiences better positions us to support both their right to learn how to read and their right to enjoy the process.

Unfortunately, when combined, Joy's studies indicate that approximately one-third of K–2 participants reported low motivation for their reading intervention program (Erickson, 2019; Erickson et al., 2020). Low motivation is unlikely to support the intervention's primary goal of furthering reading proficiency. Additionally, the 2020 study revealed that adult evaluations of 5 (out of 14) children's motivation for their reading intervention program did not align with children's self-reports.

A key implication of this work is that there are likely other young readers out there experiencing dissatisfaction. These children deserve to be identified and supported. How many children in our own care are struggling to connect to reading lessons? How many can offer suggestions for improvement? We simply cannot know the answers to these important questions without directly consulting and including the children themselves.

TEACHERS ARE INNOVATORS

In our experience, teachers care deeply about kids. They care deeply about supporting their reading development, and they care deeply about nurturing their motivation. Each and every day teachers perform motivation miracles small and large.

Over the course of the global COVID-19 pandemic, we watched teachers purchase and deliver meals to students' houses to ensure their brains were fueled to read at 8:00 a.m. We watched them "fly" and dance in character, serving as both literal and metaphorical Zoom superheroes. The two teachers pictured in Figure P.1 masterfully used their superhero personas to curb pandemic-sized emotional meltdowns threatening their young students' vital learning opportunities. And we watched teachers work tirelessly to get the books their individual students *wanted* to read into their little hands no matter where they resided.

Figure P.1. Amanda Murphy and Victoria Nixon: Two Kindergarten Zoom Superheroes

There is no question that teachers do double duty as motivation superheroes. However, to the best of our knowledge they haven't—yet—developed the ability to read minds. Can you imagine what might happen if they did?!

To truly understand how school reading programs influence individual children's motivation, we need to involve them directly in the inquiry process. We need to ask our students what they think about specific reading programs in ways that make sense to them, and we need to permit them to answer in ways that make sense to them, too. One way to thoroughly and systematically examine young children's motivation for a specific reading program is to conduct a case study.

THE POWER OF CASE STUDY

Case study is a practical research design that is well suited to generating the kind of information we aim to collect so we can understand more about our students' program-specific reading motivation. Motivation is a complex phenomenon; multiple factors typically influence an individual's motivation for any given activity.

Recall that Chrissy shared two key factors she believed to be influencing her low motivation for her reading intervention: book topic and intervention tools. Motivation research has identified numerous potential other factors that students may or may not formally recognize. These range from the quality of the relationship between the child and teacher to the amount of autonomy afforded.

A research design open to recognizing a wide range of factors potentially influencing a child's willingness to participate in a reading program better positions teachers to make changes responsive to the needs of individuals. If we narrowly examined whether our students were like Chrissy—namely, whether the books and/or word-building tiles supplied in their reading program were motivationally supportive, we might miss many additional influential factors.

We simply cannot address motivational issues if we are not aware of them. Adopting a case study approach to study children's program-specific motivation empowers teachers to make changes to reading programming that are responsive to children's *individual* needs.

We urge you to begin examining your students' reading motivation if you have not done so already and to continue this important work if it has already been a part of your practice. To support your efforts, we offer this start-to-finish and step-by-step interactive guide to conducting case studies of children's reading motivation.

Because many young children struggle to understand and respond to traditional research methods (e.g., surveys), this text places a heavy emphasis on collecting and making sense of qualitative data. However, relevant and meaningful opportunities for collecting and interpreting developmentally appropriate quantitative measures of reading motivation are also included. In sum, you will find what you need here to begin thoughtfully and systematically examining *your* students' reading motivation.

We hope, too, that you will find guidance and encouragement from voices much like your own—from people who care deeply about kids, reading, and the beautiful, catalyzing relationship that can exist between them both.

REFERENCES

Erickson, J. D. (2019). Primary students' emic views of reading intervention: A qualitative case study of motivation. *Literacy Research: Theory, Method, and Practice, 68*(1), 86–107.

Erickson, J. D., Condie, C., & Wharton-McDonald, R. (2020). Harnessing the power of young children's perceptions to support motivation. *The Reading Teacher, 73*(6), 777–787.

Hatch, J. A. (2012). Introduction. In G. Perry, B. Henderson, & D. R. Meier, *Our inquiry, our practice: Undertaking, supporting, and learning from early childhood research(ers)* (p. ix). NAEYC Books.

Ritchhart, R., Church, M., & Morrison, K. (2011). *Making thinking visible: How to promote engagement, understanding, and independence for all learners*. John Wiley & Sons.

Acknowledgments

So many people have supported me the past seven years as I worked toward completing this text. First, I thank my husband, Ryan, and my parents, Susan and William, for being constant sources of unconditional love, encouragement, and childcare. I am also immensely appreciative for, and in awe of, my wonderful daughter, Gabriella Reese—the true inspiration for this work.

I sincerely thank the chair of my dissertation committee (Ruth Wharton-McDonald), the committee members (Winston C. Thompson, Cami Condie, Paula Salvio, and Michael Middleton), and my Literacy Research Association mentor (Seth Parsons) for their guidance, time, and feedback on the earliest iterations of this project. Additionally, I wish to express my thanks to the many professors with whom I learned at the University of New Hampshire including Andrew Coppens, Todd DeMitchell, Judy Sharkey, and Suzanne Graham.

I owe much gratitude to Tom Koerner and Kira Hall of Rowman & Littlefield and to my colleague, Luke Reynolds, for kindly and compassionately helping me navigate the publication process. Portions of this project were funded by the University of New Hampshire and Endicott College; I am extremely appreciative of this financial support.

Finally, I express my sincere thanks to the children and educators who welcomed me into their communities; shared their processes, ideas, and views; and engaged in research with me as partners. Without them, this book and its impact would not be possible.

Introduction

We all should care about increasing children's motivation for school reading programs in part because we sincerely want them to succeed academically. High motivation for reading clearly supports acquisition of the skills necessary to read well. Being able to read well supports college and career success, which, in turn, has a profound impact on one's quality of life. Children's early reading experiences, then, should be largely positive for the sake of short-term and long-term outcomes.

At the same time, of equal importance is honoring the in-the-moment humanity of each child served by the reading program. Children deserve to enjoy and feel efficacious about their early reading experiences; positive self-perceptions nurture developing identities. To better ensure that young readers do enjoy and feel efficacious within their reading programs, the adults overseeing and/or implementing these programs have an obligation to carefully examine children's perceptions of the reading programs they experience.

In all other United Nations (UN) member countries, children's rights to express their views on *all* matters impacting them and to have those views taken seriously are recognized by international law (United Nations Treaty Collection, n.d.). The United States remains the sole UN member country not to ratify the Convention on the Rights of the Child—the international agreement that protects these rights.

Additionally, there is currently a concentrated focus in the United States on screening for early indicators of reading difficulties and progress monitoring the development of foundational reading skills. To be sure, early screening and progress monitoring are extremely important. However, it is equally important to recognize the role that motivation plays in learning how to read and in developing and sustaining a reading habit. Rarely are U.S. schools required or even encouraged to screen for low reading motivation, let alone routinely monitor children's reading motivation.

Two related potential explanations for the lack of attention to children's developing motivation include that adults believe they already know how children are experiencing reading programs and that adults believe the children served by these programs are largely satisfied with them. A less generous possible explanation might be that those in power are not especially concerned about children's perceived satisfaction of school reading programs. All three explanations are unacceptable.

Though many school leaders and educators in the United States are not required by international law or encouraged by national and district policies to probe children's school reading experiences or take them seriously, many find themselves moved to do so by their own moral code. The contributors of this text and I are among them. Whether your own reasons for engaging with this book are skill related, identity related, or a combination of the two, the chapters that follow will support you in examining children's motivation for specific school reading programs.

The case study approach detailed here reflects the knowledge my collaborators and I have accumulated over our past six years conducting and/or analyzing case studies of reading motivation with K–2 readers. I have had the great privilege and honor of discussing a variety of reading intervention programs with 5- through 7-year-olds across the northeastern portion of the United States. The insights and innovations of the children—who were all labeled "struggling readers" and many also labeled "English Language Learners"—shaped the iteration of the case study method presented in this text. Each chapter is framed by a child's voice in the form of a quotation.

Reading Motivation: A Guide to Understanding and Supporting Children's Willingness to Read is a step-by-step, start-to-finish guide for completing rigorous yet practical case studies of K–2 students' motivation for a specific reading program. It offers a systematic process that individuals—and better yet, teams—can utilize to learn more about how the students they serve are experiencing their reading program. The insight gained from children's own understandings can then be used to better support their motivation, engagement, and skill acquisition within these programs. The method is divided among 10 main chapters.

Chapter 1 invites you to do some soul-searching before getting to work. After defining motivation and explaining the role it plays in becoming a proficient reader, this first chapter explains why it is imperative that we consider children's own understandings of reading programs. Additionally, it rectifies three pervasive false assumptions about young children's developing reading motivation that may dissuade some from paying attention to it. A final exercise supports you in determining whether conducting case studies of motivation is for you.

Chapter 2 offers an overview of case study methodology. Important terms are defined in an accessible manner. You are assisted in identifying an individual or small group of children to study and drafting an overarching inquiry question.

Chapter 3 supports you in synthesizing relevant literature for your study. This chapter makes the process less nebulous than others because of its laser focus on reading motivation. Influential reading motivation scholars and their foundational findings are summarized from which you can tailor your own literature review.

Chapter 4 introduces multiple types of data used in motivation case study work (e.g., field notes, reflective journal entries, student interviews). You will learn how to go about selecting the types of data you will collect and how to collect them in relation to your research question(s). You will also learn how to bolster the trustworthiness of your findings through your selections. Additionally, Chapter 4 offers tips on how to collect data in ethically sound ways.

Chapter 5 supports busy teachers in planning for data collection. The daily schedule of Kyleigh Rousseau, a kindergarten teacher, is deconstructed to make visible places where data collection might occur. An initial time line for collecting the data Kyleigh might need to answer her research questions is outlined and discussed.

In Chapter 6 you will learn how to create a plan for analyzing your data. The chapter clarifies differences between formative and summative types of data analysis in relation to qualitative and quantitative data, and it shares a plan for analyzing Kyleigh's data.

Chapters 7 and 8 describe how to go about analyzing qualitative and quantitative data, respectively. Practical examples explaining how to complete formative and summative forms of qualitative data analysis are offered in Chapter 7, while Chapter 8 illustrates how to use Excel to generate simple descriptive statistics (e.g., mean, standard deviation) from survey data gathered at the beginning and end of a study.

Chapter 9 discusses some of the potential benefits of sharing your findings within and beyond your school community, and it offers tips for sharing with different audiences.

Chapter 10 describes how other educators have changed their practice in accordance with findings from case studies of their students' program-specific motivation. The chapter emphasizes the potential for improving practice and maximizing students' enjoyment of school reading programs as a result of an ongoing inquiry process.

The text concludes with a discussion of what might be. The epilogue asks you to imagine the possibilities of reading programs that make good use of reading science and students' own motivation-related perceptions.

It is the contributors' and my hope that this text will support you in reimagining reading programs in ways that better support the developing motivation of your students. We would love to hear about how you have used this text to support your students' reading motivation. If at any point in your journey you are moved to share your progress, process, findings, and/or struggles, please do so by emailing Joy directly at jdangora@endicott.edu.

REFERENCES

United Nations Treaty Collection. (n.d.). *UN, United Nations, UN treaties, treaties*. Chapter IV, Human rights: 11. Convention on the rights of the child. https://treaties.un.org/Pages/ViewDetails.aspx?src=IND&mtdsg_no=IV-11&chapter=4

Chapter 1

Why Should I Probe My Students' Program-Specific Motivation?

Joy Dangora Erickson

> "So, it's OK for me to say what I um, don't like to do here too?"—Sadie, age 6

Six-year-old Sadie asked her interviewer this question after the interviewer shared that she was trying to learn more about what kids liked and didn't like about their reading intervention program. "Cause my teacher says we should keep what we don't like about something in our heart of hearts so that we don't make people sad," Sadie continued.

The interviewer thanked Sadie for her concern for others and assured her that she would not be making anyone sad by sharing her thoughts. She went on to explain that the only way they could try and make the intervention even more fun and interesting was to know more about what kids like her thought about it. Sadie was satisfied with this explanation and went on to share her views. What she appreciated about the intervention and what she problematized were later used to make small adjustments to it.

It should be more than OK for all of our students to tell us what they understand to be working or not working in their specific school reading programs. Voicing their opinions and ideas should be highly encouraged if our sincere goal is to maximize learning. The evidence is clear: motivation supports the engagement necessary for short-term and long-term learning (Guthrie & Wigfield, 2017). Children's early experiences with text can have a profound impact on whether they choose to replace regularly and actively in reading and related activities (Willingham, 2017).

How are we to really know whether our students feel successful, enjoy, and value *their* reading programs if we do not consult them? Nearly everyone agrees that reading programs—designed by adults—will not interest and/or work for all children. If this is such an obvious and inevitable outcome, why are we not spending more time and energy probing children's own perceptions of school reading programs? By conducting case studies of students' motivation specific to their reading program(s), we are amplifying their voices and, in turn, supporting their development.

"Motivation deals with the whys of behavior; motivation theorists try to understand the choices individuals make about which activity to do or not to do" (Wigfield, 1997, p. 14). When we conduct case studies of students' motivation specific to one or more school reading programs, we are essentially acting as reading motivation theorists.

However, unlike those whose primary line of work is educational research, reading instructors are in a unique position to better understand their students' motivation. Teachers have more access to students than many researchers do, have built trusting relationships with them, and have a vested interest in students successes and their own. Reading instructors are well positioned to examine students motivation *with* them and make thoughtful adjustments to practice and programming.

Additionally, by studying students' motivation for specific reading programs, we can make a valuable contribution to the field. The voices of educators and young children are underrepresented in the scholarly literature. By sharing findings with other stakeholders and the reading motivation community, we are amplifying voices that have largely gone unheard.

WHY STUDY YOUNG CHILDREN'S MOTIVATION?

You may be asking yourself, "But why not focus on achievement?" The answer to this question is twofold. First, exclusively studying students' achievement rarely involves soliciting their feedback about the programs that are imposed upon them. Children's views of their school reading programs are not often represented in the scholarly literature.

Democratizing the process allows children to have a say in the programs in which they are required to participate. In every other United Nations (UN) member country, children's right to voice their opinions on matters impacting them is recognized by international law. As discussed in the introduction, the United States remains the sole UN member not to ratify the Convention on the Rights of the Child, which declares that children's opinions should not only be invited but also taken seriously.

Second, motivation drives engagement, which supports learning and achievement (Wigfield et al., 2015). When children enjoy and value their academic experiences, they willingly engage and exert more effort in them than they otherwise might. High levels of engagement and ample opportunities for practice promote skill acquisition. But how can you really know whether students appreciate the reading programs you provide without asking them? Students' own views of school programs are crucial for supporting their developing motivation (Kaplan et al., 2002).

Though stagnant reading achievement is commonly regarded as a significant problem in the United States and has been the focus of numerous reform efforts over the years (e.g., Reading First, U.S. Department of Education, 2003; Individuals with Disabilities Education Act, U.S. Department of Education, 2015), reforms typically fall short of adequately advocating for the cultivation of reading motivation (Pressley et al., 2007). And, unlike reading skill acquisition, they do not mandate that students' developing motivation be closely monitored or supported.

Relatedly, widely adopted academic standards including the Common Core State Standards (National Governors Association Center for Best Practices, 2010) dictate what children should be able to do at each grade level, but they fail to underscore the importance of supporting children's developing reading motivation (Shanahan, 2015). It is imperative that we find out how children are experiencing the reading programs imposed upon them to better support their motivation and skill development.

A SEVT DEFINITION OF MOTIVATION

Situated Expectancy-Value Theory, or SEVT (formerly Expectancy-Value Theory [EVT]), is a theory of motivation often used to study and explain the reading motivation of younger children, including children in kindergarten through second grade. The theory posits that students' choices, levels of persistence, and levels of performance can largely be explained by: (1) their beliefs about how well they will do on a specific task or activity (Can I do this?); and (2) the value they attach to completing it (Do I want to do this, and why?) (Wigfield, 1997; Wigfield & Eccles, 2020; Wigfield et al. 2015).

The answers to these important questions shape the degree to which children willingly participate in reading activities. The "Can I do this?" part is fairly self-explanatory; however, it is important to point out that this question, "Can I do this?" is focused directly on the task at hand—can I do this precise task (e.g., build this specific word; read this specific book)?

Though young children tend to exhibit a healthy, albeit often inflated, sense of self confidence, for example, believe that they are good readers, many will share their specific challenges with a trusted adult. For example, Chrissy, the kindergarten student discussed in the preface, explained that though she considered herself a good reader, building words with digraph letter tiles was frustrating, so much so that she listed it as a main reason for not wanting to attend intervention. When striving to understand students' motivation for a program, it may be helpful to probe expectancy beliefs for each component of the program.

The "Do I want to do this, and why?" part, or task value, has traditionally been described as consisting of three positive components. They include, (1) the intrinsic value or the enjoyment or interest a learner associates with a task, (2) the utility value or the perceived usefulness of the task, and (3) the attainment value, or the extent to which the task confirms a personally important aspect of the self.

Cost, or what a learner perceives they must give up to participate in a task (Wigfield & Eccles, 1992), is a negative component posited to influence motivation. Again, referencing Chrissy's case (described in the preface), not being able to regularly read books that interested her appeared to be depleting her motivation for/willingness to attend her reading intervention. Her own perceptions, realized by conducting a case study, led to pedagogical and content changes aimed at supporting her motivation—changes that would not have occurred otherwise.

Imagine what could be done to maximize motivation within reading programs if we knew more about children's own views. Though motivation is complex in part because there are numerous factors capable of shaping it, you might find it grounding to remember that motivation "deals with the *whys* of behavior" (Wigfield, 1997, p.14). A primary goal when conducting case studies with young readers should be to understand whether they truly enjoy and value time spent in their reading program, and why.

MOTIVATION INFLUENCES SKILL DEVELOPMENT AND ACHIEVEMENT

Studies have consistently shown that motivation matters when it comes to learning how to read well (Guthrie & Wigfield, 2017). Reading motivation has long been linked to the amount of reading children do; voracious reading supports the development of fluent reading (Stanovich, 1986).

More recently, scholars have shown that motivation supports individual components of younger children's reading. For example, Schiefele and colleagues (2016), found that second- and third-grade students' reading involvement (i.e., the degree to which they got lost in their reading) was related to how much they comprehended. Arguably of particular importance for reading programs aiming to support beginning readers and those who find learning to read a challenge, Fives and colleagues (2014) found liking one's reading instruction to be positively associated with vocabulary and phonemic awareness achievement.

Similarly, Eckert and colleagues (2017) found that children's positive valuing of a literacy intervention promoted their academic achievement. Students who mainly valued their writing intervention tended to make more progress in learning to write than those who did not. Scanlon and colleagues (2017) emphasize that "attention to children's motivation for reading and writing is especially important in discussions of RTI [Response to Intervention] because it is widely recognized that individuals who find learning challenging are apt to try to avoid those situations" (p. 55).

But how often is adequate attention being paid to children's developing motivation within reading programs including intervention programs? If the scholarly literature serves as an indicator, it is safe to say not nearly enough. If we want to support children in developing reading proficiency as efficiently as possible, we would be wise to invest more time and resources in understanding and supporting their developing motivation within reading programs. So, what might be holding us back from doing this?

An intense emphasis on meeting grade-level reading benchmarks is one fairly obvious potential factor. Though the controversy surrounding an increased focus on academics in the early years is not the focus of this text, it should be clear by now that monitoring and supporting students' individual motivation for reading programs functions to support their meeting high academic standards while nurturing their more holistic well-being (e.g., need for autonomy, happiness). Other erroneous assumptions about reading programs and younger children may also be serving as deterrents.

Three Myths About Young Children and Reading Instruction

Pervasive myths about young children's capabilities and/or reading instruction remain more prevalent than we might like to think. Such myths may be dissuading educators and researchers alike from listening to the children they serve and from digging deeper into their motivation-related perceptions of school reading programs.

Common myths include: (1) young children offer inaccurate information about school programming, (2) there is no need to talk to children because adults can easily gauge children's engagement and motivation, and (3) children's reading motivation will improve when their reading skill improves, so low short-term motivation does not matter all that much. In the sections below, each one of these problematic false claims is dismantled in hopes of demythifying them for the sake of children's developing reading motivation.

Myth #1: Young Children Cannot Be Trusted to Answer and/ or Do Not Understand What Is Being Asked of Them

"But how do you know you can trust what the kids are telling you?" is unfortunately an all too common question posed when sharing children's perceptions about their learning experiences with adults. To some degree, you might be able to sympathize with those who question children's trustworthiness. You can likely recall at least one instance where a child told you or someone else a total whopper. But are children really any more likely to lie than adults? And if so, is it so much so that we should ignore their views of school?

In the first study of its kind—a cross-sectional examination of lying across the lifespan (ages 6–77)—Debey and colleagues (2015) found that teenagers in a sample of more than 1,000 people were more likely to lie than all other age groups. The youngest participants, 6-year-olds, were among the least likely to mislead others.

So, sure children may tell a fib now and again, but there simply is not a strong empirical basis for believing they are any more likely to do so than adults. And, when they do lie, children's lies are typically easier to spot than those of adults. Put plainly, a lack of faith in children's trustworthiness is not a sufficient reason for failing to probe and sincerely consider their own perceptions of school reading programs—or any other program for that matter.

"But, isn't it true that children are likely to misunderstand what is being asked of them, thus rendering their responses futile?" is an iteration of another critique of children's abilities to report their views and understandings. It is true that young children's capacities to understand and express language are certainly not as mature as adults. So, then is it worth asking them about their motivation if they might struggle to comprehend and/or answer questions? The answer to this question is unequivocally, YES.

Numerous studies have successfully overcome challenges posed by children's less mature language capacities. Most involve making good use of materials and language that makes sense to the children involved in the project. For example, Measelle and colleagues (1998) used puppets and incorporated children's own speaking styles into the study they designed to probe children's perceptions of school adjustment.

They also invited the children in the study to respond to questions with words and/or by pointing to images. The adults leading the research project remained flexible in their use of developmentally appropriate techniques to support children's comprehension and expression throughout the inquiry process. Many other studies (e.g., Clark & Moss, 2001; Daniels et al., 2001;

Harris, 2015) have also successfully overcome children's potential language limitations by using participatory research methods.

Participatory methods encourage children to take a more autonomous role in the research process. Examples of participatory research techniques include permitting children to operate recording devices and to take the lead during interviews (e.g., student-led walking-tour interviews). Who better to reimagine research techniques in developmentally appropriate ways than teachers?

Teachers regularly adjust their language to ensure children understand what is being asked, and they are well versed in their students' own speaking styles. Furthermore, they regularly make use of multiple modes of expression and encourage multiple modes of representation. Early childhood teachers may be better positioned to make good use of children's linguistic strengths while supporting their needs in an interview situation than many—if not most—researchers. A lack of faith in children's language capabilities is also not a sufficient reason for failing to probe and consider children's perceptions.

Myth #2: Adults Can Accurately Gauge Children's Willingness to Participate in Activities

Another common misconception is that adults "know" when children are engaged or not engaged in school activities as well as whether they are participating willingly in reading programs. Some claim it is easy to tell this based on listening to children's utterances and watching their behaviors and body language in class. Of course, this is true to some extent: when a child shuts down, starts to cry, throws something, or storms out of the room, it's fairly safe to assume that the child is not enjoying participating in the task at hand.

But, what about a highly distractible student? Is a distracted student always an unmotivated one? Certainly, there are times when a child who largely enjoys reading time cannot help but become distracted by peers, noises, smells, an upset stomach, or something else. Though the child may be frequently distracted, their motivation for the reading program may be largely positive.

On the other end of the spectrum, might a child who really does not enjoy participating in a reading program regularly comply with the teacher's requests to please one or more adults (e.g., parent, teacher) and/or to avoid punishment, thus giving the appearance of being an engaged and motivated participant? Studies centering on the United Kingdom's imposed National Reading Curriculum (e.g., Pollard & Triggs, 2000) have found that teachers' perceptions of elementary students' motivation and students' self-reported motivation do not always match.

Specific to research involving young K–2 readers, instances of children appearing largely engaged but reporting low motivation for their reading intervention and instances of children exhibiting low engagement and reporting high motivation for their intervention program exist in the literature (Erickson, 2019; Erickson et al., 2020). Chrissy's case, detailed in the preface of this text, is a prime example of how we might mistake a child's compliance for high motivation.

More important, through conducting developmentally appropriate participatory interviews with Chrissy, the research team was able to identify aspects of the reading intervention that could easily be changed (without sacrificing the program's scope and sequence or evidence-based drills) to better support her motivation. These included incorporating more connected texts that centered on her interests and permitting her to use individual letter tiles to form digraphs.

We are left with two key takeaways. First, we should not assume we "know" the degree to which a child is motivated or not to participate in their reading program(s). And second, probing children's program-specific motivation may offer important insights that permit us to better support their unique motivation.

Myth #3: Children's Reading Motivation Automatically Improves as Children Become More Skilled

It is true that reading motivation and reading achievement are related. Regardless of age, more proficient readers tend to report enjoying reading more than those who are less skilled (for a review see Morgan and Fuchs, 2007). However, you likely know at least one person who reads well enough but claims not to enjoy reading. Of those who largely dislike reading, many attribute a portion of their disdain to negative school experiences. The stigma of being placed and tracked in a "low" reading group is one rationale many adults offer.

According to Willingham (2017) and others, children's early reading experiences play a pivotal role in shaping their reading motivation. Surely school experiences as well as home experiences shape children's decisions of whether to engage in reading and related activities. Empirical evidence also suggests that younger children do not always enjoy reading upon gaining higher levels of reading proficiency.

Morgan, Fuchs, Compton, et al. (2008), for example, found that "at-risk" first grade students' statistically significant reading improvement following an evidence-based reading intervention did not lead to significant increases in reading motivation. In response to this finding, Morgan, Fuchs, Compton, et al. (2008) emphasized the need to more directly support children's motivation within early reading programs.

While some reading programs may be designed with motivation in mind, many evidence-based reading programs are generally supported by evidence demonstrating their effectiveness in terms of foundational skill building, not their effectiveness for boosting motivation. Additionally, each child's motivation for reading in general and the reading program(s) they are enrolled in is unique—one size simply doesn't fit all.

There are far too many factors capable of influencing motivation than can be accounted for in a single program. Therefore, it is imperative that we examine and support individual readers' motivation specific to their reading program(s). It is not safe to assume that any program or gain in foundational reading skills will automatically lead to enhanced reading motivation.

SUMMARY

This text draws heavily upon the Situated Expectancy-Value Theory of motivation to understand young children's motivation to read. SEVT suggests that students' choices, levels of persistence, and levels of performance can largely be explained by (a) their beliefs about how well they will do specific to a task or activity (Can I do this?); and (b) the value they attach to completing it (Do I want to do this, and why?).

All stakeholders should care about children's motivation specific to their school reading programs because motivation has been shown time and time again to relate to learners' short-term and long-term reading outcomes. The experiences children have at school can influence their willingness to engage in reading. It is important to elicit and sincerely consider children's own perceptions of school programs because their self reports do not always match adult assumptions.

Stakeholders need not let concern for the trustworthiness of children's responses hold them back from examining children's motivation. Research indicates that young children are generally at least as trustworthy as older learners. Lastly, children's motivation should be regularly monitored and specifically targeted because improvements in reading skill do not always equate to improvements in reading motivation.

REFERENCES

Clark, A., & Moss, P. (2001). *Listening to young children: The mosaic approach.* National Children's Bureau.

Table 1.1. Activity 1

Soul Searching Exercise: Is This Worth My Time?
Do I believe that reading motivation is underemphasized in my classroom, school, district, state, and/or federal reform initiatives? Y/N?
Yes because: **No** because:
Are there students in my care who stand to benefit from me more closely examining their motivation for a specific reading experience (e.g., core reading program, reading intervention)? Y/N
YES because (include students' names)   Figure 1.1. *James Dangora*   **NO** because: 
Given my answers to these questions, **I am/am not** (circle one) willing to examine my students' reading motivation at this time. Notes:

Daniels, D. H., Kalkman, D. L., & McCombs, B. L. (2001). Young children's perspectives on learning and teacher practices in different classroom contexts: Implications for motivation. *Early Education and Development, 12*(2), 253–273.

Debey, E., De Schryver, M., Logan, G. D., Suchotzki, K., & Verschuere, B. (2015). From junior to senior Pinocchio: A cross-sectional lifespan investigation of deception. *Acta Psychologica*, 160, 58–68. https://doi_org.unh.idm.oclc.org/10.1016/j.actpsy.2015.06.007

Eckert, T. L., Hier, B. O., Hamsho, N. F., & Malandrino, R. D. (2017). Assessing children's perceptions of academic interventions: The kids intervention profile. *School Psychology Quarterly, 32*(2), 268–281. https://doi.org/10.1037/spq0000200

Erickson, J. D. (2019). Primary students' emic views of reading intervention: A qualitative case study of motivation. *Literacy Research: Theory, Method, and Practice, 68*(1), 86–107.

Erickson, J. D., Condie, C., & Wharton-McDonald, R. (2020). Harnessing the power of young children's perceptions to support motivation. *The Reading Teacher, 73*(6), 777–787.

Fives, A., Russell, D., Kearns, N., Lyons, R., Eaton, P., Canavan, J., Devaney, C., & O'Brien, A. (2014). The association between academic self-beliefs and reading achievement among children at risk of reading failure. *Journal of Research in Reading, 37*(2), 215–232.

Guthrie, J. T., & Wigfield, A. (2017). Literacy engagement and motivation: Rationale, research, teaching, and assessment. In D. Lapp & D. Fisher (Eds.), *Handbook of research on teaching the English Language Arts*. Routledge. https://doi.org/10.4324/9780203839713.ch3

Harris, P. (2015). "Words and stuff": Exploring children's perspectives of classroom reading in the early school years. *Australian Journal of Language and Literacy, 38*(1), 27–37.

Kaplan, A., Middleton, M. J., Urdan, T., & Midgley, C. (2002). Achievement goals and goal structures. In C. Midgley (Ed.), *Goals, goal structures, and patterns of adaptive learning* (pp. 21–53). Lawrence Erlbaum Associates.

Measelle, J. R., Ablow, J. C., Cowan, P. A., & Cowan, C. P. (1998). Assessing young children's views of their academic, social, and emotional lives: An evaluation of the self-perception scales of the Berkeley Puppet Interview. *Child Development, 69*(6), 1556–1576.

Morgan, P. L., & Fuchs, D (2007). Is there a bidirectional relationship between children's reading skills and reading motivation? *Exceptional Children, 73*(2), 165–183.

Morgan, P. L., Fuchs, D., Compton, D. L., Cordray, D. S., & Fuchs, L. S. (2008). Does early reading failure decrease children's reading motivation? *Journal of Learning Disabilities, 41*(5), 387–404. https://doi.org/10.1177/0022219408321112

National Governors Association Center for Best Practices, Council of Chief State School Officers. (2010). *Common Core State Standards for English Language Arts*. National Governors Association Center for Best Practices, Council of Chief State School Officers.

Pollard, A., & Triggs, P. (2000). *What pupils say: Changing policy and practice in primary education*. Continuum.

Pressley, M., Billman, A. K., Perry, K. H., Reffitt, K. E., & Reynolds, J. M. (2007). *Shaping literacy achievement: Research we have, research we need*. Guilford.

Scanlon, D. M., Anderson, K. L., & Sweeney, J. M. (2017). *Early intervention for reading difficulties: The interactive strategies approach*. Guilford.

Schiefele, U., Stutz, F., & Schaffner, E. (2016). Longitudinal relations between reading motivation and reading comprehension in the early elementary grades. *Learning and Individual Differences, 51*, 49–58. https://doi.org/10.1016/j.lindif.2016.08.031

Shanahan, T. (2015). What teachers should know about Common Core: A guide for the perplexed. *The Reading Teacher, 68*(8), 583–588.

Stanovich, K. E. (1986). Matthew effects in reading: Some consequences of individual differences in the acquisition of literacy. *Reading Research Quarterly, 21*(4), 360–407.

Wigfield, A. (1997). Children's motivations for reading and writing engagement. In J. T. Guthrie & A. Wigfield (Eds.), *Reading engagement: Motivating readers through integrated instruction* (pp. 14–33). International Reading Association.

Wigfield, A., & Eccles, J. S. (1992). The development of achievement task values: A theoretical analysis. *Developmental Review, 12*(3), 265–310.

Wigfield, A., & Eccles, J. S. (2020). 35 years of research on students' subjective task values and motivation: A look back and a look forward. In A. J. Elliot (Ed.), *Advances in motivation science* (Vol. 7, pp. 161–198). Elsevier Academic Press.

Wigfield, A., Eccles, J. S., Fredricks, J. A., Simpkins, S., Roeser, R. W., & Schiefele, U. (2015). Development of achievement motivation and engagement. In M. E. Lamb & M. Lerner (Eds.), *Handbook of child psychology and developmental science: Socioemotional processes* (7th ed., pp. 657–700). John Wiley & Sons.

Willingham, D. T. (2017). *The reading mind: A cognitive approach to understanding how the mind reads.* Jossey-Bass.

Chapter 2

OK, OK, I'm In! Now What?!

Defining Your Case and Refining Your Inquiry Question

Joy Dangora Erickson and Beth Fornauf

> "We all do the same thing. . . . First we do a check-in, then we read old books, then we do sounds and trick words, and then we do boards."—Daniel, age 6

Daniel was one of three first-grade students participating for a second year in a case study aimed at better understanding each child's motivation for a specific reading intervention program. All students involved in the study clearly and accurately described what happened in their intervention the first year (in kindergarten) and the second year (in first grade). As discussed in Chapter 1, some adults are skeptical of the trustworthiness of children's self-reports. Asking children to describe what typically occurs in a program and comparing their responses to your own or other knowledgeable adults' understandings may mitigate such concerns.

A major advantage of a case study approach to doing research is that it is extremely flexible in this way. You can probe and elicit younger children's views in relation to a specific inquiry question and then collect additional data from other sources to compare responses. Though scholars have yet to rally around a single definition of the case study approach, case studies can be readily identified by their hallmark features.

Creswell and Poth (2018) refer to each of these features when they describe case study methodology as "a qualitative approach in which the investigator explores a real-life, contemporary bounded system (a case) or multiple bounded systems (cases) over time, through detailed, in-depth data collection involving *multiple sources of information* (e.g., observations, interviews, audiovisual material, and documents and reports), and reports a *case description* and *case themes* " (p. 96–97; emphasis in original). Let's take a moment to extract and discuss each key feature.

THE QUALITATIVE NATURE OF CASE STUDY WORK

Though case study work can incorporate numerically based quantitative methods, it often relies heavily on the use of qualitative methods. Qualitative methods typically involve collecting, analyzing, and making sense of non-numerical data (e.g., interview transcripts, diary entries)—namely, words (Braun and Clarke, 2013). Qualitative methods can be especially useful when striving to better *understand* a complex phenomenon like a person's motivation for an activity. They can also be helpful when working with individuals who experience difficulty expressing their views and/or understandings through more traditional means, like surveys.

Because you are interested in understanding more about young readers' motivation for a specific program, qualitative research methods are often advantageous. You will likely want to know what each student appreciates about the program, what they do not, and their rationales for both. Previously validated numerical surveys of motivation rarely collect this kind of program-specific information, and when they do, children are forced to fit their responses to one of the choices offered. Additionally, younger students can struggle to read, comprehend, and/or complete traditional surveys on their own.

It can be more feasible and can yield more trustworthy results to converse with children about their reading program in ways that make good sense to them (e.g., while drawing or touring the space where they do the reading). You may elect to use qualitative methods in combination with a quantitative measure of overall reading motivation. Such a decision could support an inquiry aimed at better understanding students' program-specific motivation as well as their more general motivation to read.

Though not always helpful for understanding a young reader's motivation for a specific program, the *Me and My Reading Profile* (MMRP; Marinak et al., 2015) is an example of a validated survey suitable for measuring K–2 children's overall motivation to read. If you suspect your inquiry might benefit from the use of this tool or a similar one, additional information explaining how to use the MMRP and how to interpret and report results from it can be found in Chapters 4 and 8, respectively.

Even when your inquiry makes good use of a reputable quantitative tool like the MMRP, using a case study approach, like most other forms of qualitative research, typically involves you (or your team) functioning as the primary data collection and sense-making instrument (Merriam & Tisdell, 2016). You or your team will be primarily responsible for designing, implementing, interpreting, and reporting findings from your study.

THE REAL-LIFE CONTEMPORARY BOUNDED SYSTEM(S) REQUIREMENT

Another critical component of case study work is zeroing in on the "object of study" or the case (Merriam & Tisdell, 2016, p. 38). There must be clear limits on what you will study and why. Put differently, imagine yourself as a surveyor marking out property lines; the lines must be clearly drawn to ensure the building can be constructed well within them. The same is true for case study work.

You must be able to precisely define your case in order to determine how to go about studying it in a thorough way. One particular child, a small group of children, or an entire class are all potential cases for study. However, you must also have a clear rationale for studying each one. For example, perhaps you have noticed that one particular child appears to struggle more than others to engage in your daily reading whole group lesson. You decide to draw an imaginary boundary around this child during this time; you have identified your real-life object of study as well as your rationale for study (see Figure 2.1.a, example 1).

Another boundary might be drawn around three students you pull to the back table each week for small group work (see Figure 2.1.a., example 2). They appear mostly engaged in their reading lessons, but you wonder whether you could do more to increase their enthusiasm for reading time. You have identified a new object of study and a new (related) rationale. In both cases, you are interested in learning more about children's motivation for a specific reading program.

In one final example (see Figure 2.1.b, example 3), perhaps you decide to draw a boundary around your entire class during basal reading time. You have launched a new basal program, and you are interested to know whether most students are enjoying it and what you might do to better support their engagement. In this instance, the program can be identified as the central case; however, as you progress in the research, you decide to take a closer look at the motivation of one or more individual students. This would be an example of a case study (individual child or group) within a larger case study (program).

It is not at all uncommon for case studies to birth additional case studies. After simultaneously completing three case studies of children's motivation for a specific reading intervention program (a kindergarten group, a

Example 1

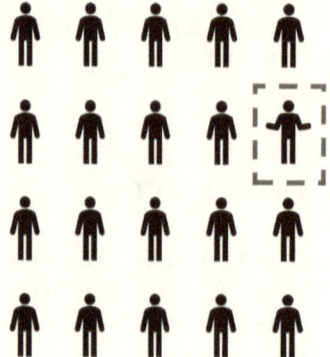

Case study exploring one student in a reading workshop who appears to be struggling

Example 2

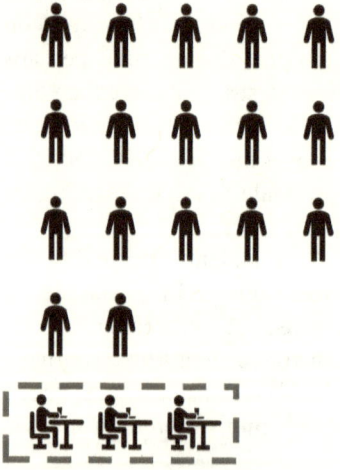

Case study exploring three students' enthusiasm for guided reading

Figure 2.1.a. Case Examples

first-grade group, and a second-grade group), Erickson and colleagues (2020) decided to follow the kindergarten students for another year. The researchers were interested in knowing whether their motivation for the intervention program would change the second year. Do not be surprised if you find yourself in a similar situation; doing research generally surfaces even more (good) questions!

Example 3

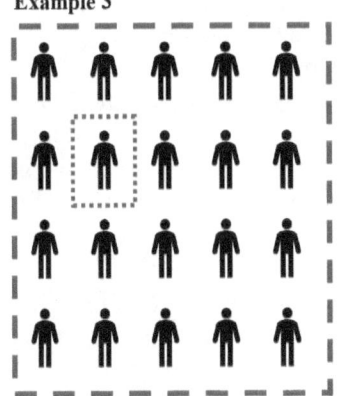

Central case exploring how to promote engagement of class in new basal reading program, and individual case of one student's motivation

Figure 2.1.b. Case Examples Continued

AN IN-DEPTH COLLECTION OF DATA ACROSS SOURCES AND TYPES OF INFORMATION

A third common feature across case studies is the amount of data collected and analyzed. Unlike survey research, which typically involves analyzing and reporting results from one specific tool and so can be completed rather quickly, case study work involves collecting and analyzing multiple types of data from multiple sources. Collecting enough data to offer a detailed account of the case takes time, usually at least several months. Extensive data collection is necessary to offer a rich description and thorough understanding of the case (Creswell & Poth, 2018; Hancock & Algozzine, 2011).

Each child's motivation for a particular reading program is different, and *many* factors (e.g., relationship with the teacher, interest in the topic, peer relationships) could be influencing it. In order to offer trustworthy findings and conclusions, you must look for patterns and discrepancies in the data. This is done by collecting relevant data from multiple sources. For example, an interviewer might ask a child who has willingly agreed to participate in the interview whether they would attend their reading intervention program if afforded the choice. If they answer affirmatively, the interviewer might follow up by asking them why.

The rationale offered can then be compared to what you observe during the intervention. For example, if the child reports enjoying the books read within the intervention, you might review your daily diary entries for comparison.

Perhaps on one occasion you noted the child's enthusiastic response when transitioning to reading time. Perhaps you repeatedly noted how engrossed the child appeared while reading intervention books.

Additionally, the child produced a drawing in which they are reading a favorite intervention book. Because the evidence from all sources (child, teacher) appears to converge, you feel confident that the books available in the reading intervention program are supporting the child's motivation for participating in the intervention. A quantitative survey of the child's overall motivation might complement your findings and conclusions.

If you conduct a pre and post measurement of the child's overall reading motivation and find that their motivation for reading in general has improved, you can claim with greater confidence that the reading intervention is unlikely to be harming the child's overall motivation to read and hypothesize that it may even be supporting it. Generally the more converging evidence you have, the more trustworthy your resultant findings and conclusions are. It is for this reason that case studies involve collecting multiple types of qualitative data (e.g., artifacts, interviews) from multiple sources (e.g., teacher, child).

RESULTANT DESCRIPTION AND THEMES

Because case studies typically involve collecting a large amount of qualitative data in a natural setting, they are capable of yielding a rich description grounded in participants' own understandings (Hancock & Algozzine, 2011). This is exciting when striving to better understand children's motivation for a specific reading program. As mentioned earlier, motivation can be shaped by a host of factors. Quantitative instruments including surveys can limit which factors are uncovered; it is not feasible to include all potential factors on a survey. This limitation increases the possibility of missing an influential motivator or demotivator.

Conducting multiple interviews with child participants during which they discuss their reasons for wanting to participate or not wanting to participate in a given program and then combining these interviews with your own observations and/or the observations of others permits offering a more comprehensive understanding of each child's program-specific motivation. Put differently, the varied types of data and sheer quantity of data collected yields a rich description of each child's motivation.

In order to thoroughly describe each child's or group of children's motivation for a given program, you must first identify pertinent themes residing in the large amount of data collected. Say, for example, you decide to study one particular child whom you suspect has low motivation for a computer-based reading program. A trusted adult conducts multiple interviews with the child to discuss his motivation (more on how to ethically conduct interviews in Chapter 4), and observes his computer-based sessions for an extended period of time.

Combing through interview transcripts and diary entries, you discover that all sources suggest the child is more eager to participate in the intervention on days that he has had a snack immediately beforehand. This pattern might then be described as a theme for later reporting: *being able to eat right beforehand appears to support X's willingness to participate in the intervention.* Discoveries like this make up the substance of the case report produced at the end of your inquiry. Whether reporting your findings solely for yourself or for an audience, listing and describing important themes allows you to make informed changes to the child's program.

GETTING STARTED

By now you likely have some ideas about who and what your case might involve. Perhaps completing the activity at the end of Chapter 1 sparked your interest in better understanding the reading motivation of one particular student. Perhaps you have recently or will soon introduce your entire class to a new basal reading program or a small group to an early reading intervention. Perhaps you use a specific structured literacy intervention to tutor a child after school, and you are interested in knowing whether that child is motivated to do this important work. Any one of these ideas can launch your first case study project.

Take a moment to jot down your potential cases. It can be difficult to decide which to begin with. It may help to think about who you believe stands to benefit the most from your inquiry. Studying a child or group of children whom you suspect struggle more than others to engage might trump your eagerness to know more about the class's motivation for the new basal reader. Your deep knowledge of your students should inform the case you select for study. Additionally, it is important to remember that all research must be done in an ethical manner.

Though teachers generally do not need formal approval from a university's Institutional Review Board (IRB) to conduct practitioner research in their own classrooms (pre-service teachers often do), it is important to be mindful of children's rights and parents' rights. First and foremost, any research project must prioritize doing no harm to participants (Forster & Eperjesi,

2021). Many children enjoy being acknowledged as the experts of their lived experiences and elect to participate actively in research. However, children's involvement in your project (outside of normal classroom activities) should be entirely voluntary and confidential.

How to go about explaining your project to children and guardians and gaining parental consent and child assent will be discussed in Chapter 4. If you know ahead of time that a particular child is unlikely to want to discuss their experiences with you or another member of your research team, it would be crossing an ethical boundary to force or coerce them into talking. It is helpful to identify such children before beginning your project and think about other ways you might gauge their motivation (e.g., detailed observations). Once you have selected your bounded case, it is time to write an inquiry question.

Drafting an Inquiry Question

Typically, one's first attempt at writing an inquiry question results in a fairly broad question that requires a good amount of fine tuning. For example, you might ask, *"How is this group of students experiencing daily small group reading lessons?"* The case is clearly bounded: it involves several students and their experiences relative to your reading program. This is important. However, the question is far too broad; you want to know about the specific experiences that may be supporting or undermining each child's motivation to participate in the lessons.

A second iteration might read, *"What does this group of children appreciate about their small group reading lessons?"* Though this question is better positioned to support an examination of the children's motivation for their reading lessons, it does not make room for potential negative perceptions. It is too narrow and thus may bias your findings.

"What does this group of children understand to be the advantages and/or disadvantages of participating in their small group reading lessons?" is a third iteration that makes room for both children's positive and negative motivation-related perceptions. This question is also compatible with the Situated Expectancy-Value Theory model of motivation introduced in Chapter 1, which maintains that, like associated values, the costs individuals associate with their participation in an activity can influence their willingness to participate.

To better understand the degree to which children's perceived advantages and disadvantages may be influencing their willingness to participate in the small group reading program, you could pose second and third follow-up questions: *"If permitted to choose, would these children attend their small group reading lessons? Why or why not?"* These additional questions support the first question by offering a window into whether and how the children link perceived advantages and/or disadvantages to wanting or not wanting to participate in the small group reading lessons.

To summarize, the first inquiry question maintained the integrity of the case but was not properly tailored to the phenomenon of interest—namely, motivation. The second question did center on motivation but was biased toward positive experiences. The final set of three questions work together to identify students' perceived advantages and disadvantages of program participation while permitting the potential identification of salient influencers of children's motivation for the program.

SUMMARY

Conducting case study research provides teachers with a wealth of opportunities to explore and understand phenomena in the classroom. It is characterized by its exploration of a real-life bounded system (or case), in-depth data collection using primarily qualitative methods, and multiple sources of data that allow researchers to generate rich descriptions and themes. Drawing on multiple data sources over an extended period of time helps establish trustworthy results that can yield questions for further investigation.

When getting started with case study research, it is important to consider several factors. Begin by generating a list of possible cases and considering what the study will involve and who might benefit from the inquiry. Be especially mindful of the ethics of research; it is incumbent upon the researcher or researchers to respect the rights of participants and to do them no harm. Researchers will need to be able to explain all major components of the project to children and parents so they can elect whether or not to participate.

Once a case is established, begin the process of drafting an inquiry question. Initial questions are often too broad (lacking specificity) or too narrow (limited in scope). A strong inquiry question should examine a specific phenomenon, be compatible with theory, and clearly identify the bounded system under investigation.

Table 2.1. Activity 2

	Three Iterations Inquiry Question Exercise			
	Who?	What?	For?	Why?
1. Stake out the boundaries of your case.	I want to know more about this (individual's, group's, class's):	Motivation (i.e., willingness to actively participate)	Specific program:	Because:

Example: To what extent are Juliet and Giovanna motivated to participate in their reading group?

Write a first iteration of your inquiry question here:

2. Make it more specific.	Specifically, I want to know more about this/ these student's/students' perceived (e.g., advantages/ likes, disadvantages/dislikes, expectations for success) _____ because:		Figure 2.2. *James Dangora* 

Example: What, if any, advantages do Juliet and Giovanna associate with participation in their reading group?

Write a second iteration of your inquiry question here:

3. Evaluate whether you are interested in knowing more or less.	Am I trying to explore too much? If this is your first case study consider limiting yourself to two types of perceptions (e.g., advantages and disadvantages). Y/N	Am I exploring enough to offer an in-depth description of the case? Consider the potential limitations of examining only one type of perception. Y/N

Example: What, if any, advantages and/or disadvantages do Juliet and Giovanna associate with participation in their reading group, and would they attend if given the choice?

Write a third iteration of your inquiry question here:

REFERENCES

Braun, V., & Clarke, V. (2013). *Successful qualitative research: A practical guide for beginners*. Sage.

Creswell, J. W., & Poth, C. N. (2018). *Qualitative inquiry & research design: Choosing among five approaches* (4th ed.). Sage.

Erickson, J. D., Condie, C., & Wharton-McDonald, R. (2020). Harnessing the power of young readers' perceptions to support motivation. *The Reading Teacher, 73*(6), 777–787. https://doi.org/10.1002/trtr.1895

Forster, C., & Eperjesi, R. (2021). *Action research for student teachers* (2nd ed.). Sage.

Hancock, D. R., & Algozzine, B. (2011). *Doing case study research: A practical guide for beginning researchers* (2nd ed.). Teachers College Press.

Marinak, B. A., Malloy, J. B., Gambrell, L. B., & Mazzoni, S. A. (2015). Me and My Reading Profile: A tool for assessing early reading motivation. *The Reading Teacher, 69*(1), 51–62. https://doi.org/10.1002/trtr.1362

Merriam, S. B., & Tisdell, E. J. (2016). *Qualitative research: A guide to design and implementation* (4th ed.). Jossey-Bass.

Chapter 3

Standing on the Shoulders of Giants

Using the Work of Others to Support Your Project

Joy Dangora Erickson and Alessandra E. Ward

> "I really like it when [the reading specialist] lets me pick my own books!"—Josh, age 7

Josh revealed this perceived advantage of attending his reading intervention program to the interviewer during a walking-tour interview. The interviewer had spent weeks attending Josh's intervention and building a trusting relationship with him before asking him to share his perceived advantages and disadvantages of the program. In short, the research team concluded that not being able to read books he enjoyed was a major demotivator for Josh, and they recommended increasing the number of personally meaningful texts from which he could choose to read in the intervention program.

This finding aligns with the scholarly literature: research suggests that offering children books they deem to be especially interesting supports their motivation (Guthrie & Wigfield, 2017). It also fits with the Situated Expectancy-Value Theory (SEVT) of motivation introduced in Chapter 1. Recall that one of the major questions posited to influence motivation is "Do I want to do this, and why?"

Josh wanted to bring in books from home because he truly enjoyed reading them. Put differently, he wanted to read books he valued. Josh's views and the scholarly literature together indicate a change should be made to the intervention he is receiving—namely, that he should be offered more intrinsically motivating (i.e., personally meaningful) books within the intervention.

SURVEYING RELEVANT LITERATURE TO SUPPORT YOUR CASE STUDY

When designing, implementing, and interpreting findings from a case study of young children's motivation, it is important to be aware of (1) school, state, and/or national trends as they relate to reading motivation; (2) influential motivation scholars and their major contributions to the field; and (3) how others have successfully conducted similar research. This knowledge will support you in explaining why your study is needed, in selecting and carrying out your research methods, and in interpreting your findings. The remainder of this chapter is divided into three main sections to assist you with these goals.

- The first section can assist you in making a solid case for conducting your study and for cultivating reading motivation. Specifically, the troubling national trend of motivational decline is introduced, and several key sources indicating this trend are shared. This section can support you in articulating a rationale for your research.
- The second section introduces you to influential reading motivation scholars and their work specific to what supports children's motivation to engage in reading and related tasks. This section serves to (1) familiarize you with practices research has found to be generally supportive of reading motivation and (2) assist you in later connecting your own findings to the scholarly literature.
- The third section offers several techniques others have found helpful when probing and eliciting younger children's perceptions. This section is intended to assist you in identifying, selecting, and making good use of developmentally sensitive inquiry methods.

It is important to note that the field of reading motivation historically has not well represented the ideas and work of scholars of color (and to a lesser extent those of female scholars) when compared to the ideas and work of White male scholars. This needs to change; your work and your encouragement of others in their work can support this change.

DECLINING READING MOTIVATION: A TROUBLING TREND

It is likely that no matter your role (e.g., teacher, researcher, student teacher) you will have to justify your study and describe what you intend to do to multiple people. You will need to craft a research proposal. This can take a variety of forms and will vary depending on your audience. If completing your undergraduate or graduate degree, you will need university approval to conduct your study, which generally involves producing a more formal paper tailored to your university's Institutional Review Board (IRB) requirements.

In all roles, you will need at a minimum the approval of school leadership, parents/guardians, and child participants. These people will want and deserve to know what you intend to do and why you want to do it. This kind of proposal may take the form of a handout or a slide show. Regardless of format, it is imperative that you clearly explain why your study is needed. When a child is showing signs of struggle, the child's frustration may serve as a pillar of support for your study. Another potential pillar may be found in school, state, and/or national data.

If your state, district, or school has been collecting data on children's reading motivation, you should review that first. However, a strong case for supporting reading motivation can be made from existing empirical literature. Although many children in the United States and elsewhere begin kindergarten with enthusiasm to learn to read, their motivation tends to decline as they progress through schooling. Here are several studies and a short synthesis of their major findings you might consider incorporating into your proposal as evidence of this troubling trend:

- Archambault and colleagues (2010) found that for all 655 children in their sample, literacy ability self-concept (i.e., how capable the children perceived themselves to be in literacy-related subjects) decreased between grades 1 and 12. Children's valuing of literacy (i.e., how useful and important they perceived literacy to be) also decreased for all children in the sample.
- Similarly, Jacobs and colleagues (2003) studied 761 students' perceived self-competence for and valuing of language arts tasks from grades 1 to 12. They found that children's perceptions in both areas declined at a steady rate over the elementary years.
- Wigfield and colleagues (1997) examined the change in 615 children's beliefs about their competence and valuing (interest, usefulness, importance) specific to reading for three consecutive years. The researchers found that the children's beliefs about their competence and their

valuing of reading declined significantly in two out of three elementary cohorts; reading motivation declined from first to third grade in cohort 1 and from second to fourth grade in cohort 2.

Findings from these studies align with a larger body of literature (for a review see Wigfield et al., 2015) suggesting reading motivation often erodes across the elementary years. If you are aiming to include additional studies, you could consult the reference list of any of the three studies listed above and/or Wigfield and colleagues' (2015) larger review of the literature. Plucking studies from the reference lists of other studies, or "snowballing" can be an excellent way to identify additional studies particularly relevant to your own project (see this chapter's culminating exercise for more information on this technique).

You could also conduct your own search using a reputable scholarly research database (e.g., EBSCOhost, Google Scholar). If you are a university student, you have access to these tools through your university library system. Many school districts also have licenses. Finally, your public library is another place you can access reputable research databases.

If you are new to conducting searches, you might begin by entering in the phrase, "development of reading motivation" and/or "changes in reading motivation," along with the specific age range or grade level(s) you are interested in studying into the search engine. Be sure to keep a record of your search terms; if you end up publishing your study in a research journal, you will want to disclose which terms and phrases you used to conduct your search.

It is also advisable to organize any studies you might use to support your project in an electronic table. At a minimum, your table should include: (1) a complete citation for each study, (2) each study's abstract *or* a summary of major findings, and (3) a topic label to support you in grouping studies by category. For example, all included studies having to do with the decline of reading motivation in elementary school might be labeled "declining reading motivation." Relatedly, it is helpful to set up electronic folders with these topic labels to house the actual studies.

INFLUENTIAL READING MOTIVATION SCHOLARS AND THEIR CONTRIBUTIONS TO THE FIELD

The degree to which a student is motivated to read and/or participate in reading-related tasks can be influenced by many factors. The SEVT model of motivation centered in this text emphasizes the role one's beliefs about performing the task and their valuing of the task play in shaping their willingness to try and exert effort (Wigfield, 1997). Relatedly, whether and how much a student perceives a task to be aligned with their personal goals (e.g., learning to read, knowing more about dinosaurs) often influences their motivation (Guthrie & Wigfield, 2017).

Numerous scholars have contributed to our collective knowledge of what generally supports reading motivation. You will want to have a sufficient level of familiarity with their work so that you can refer to relevant aspects of it in your rationale for conducting your study and/or when explaining your findings. In an effort to offer a concise foundational introduction to this extensive body of literature and some of the influential scholars associated with it, this section is largely organized by Guthrie and Wigfield's (2017) SMILE acronym.

John T. Guthrie and *Allan Wigfield,* professors emeritus at the University of Maryland at College Park, created the SMILE acronym, which organizes many known influencers of motivation into four main categories. They also offer a fifth category to consider one's cognitive, affective, and behavioral involvement in an activity, in essence, engagement relative to their motivation. The five dimensions of Guthrie and Wigfield's SMILE acronym are as follows:

- S = Sharing: Children are social beings; they benefit in many ways from sharing meaningful experiences with others. Psychologists *Edward Deci* and *Richard Ryan* at the University of Rochester describe forging and maintaining positive social relationships as a basic psychological need that when met supports motivation (Deci & Ryan, 2002).

    Peer collaboration can address this need and, in doing so, promote students' engagement in "*deeper* reading" experiences (Barber & Klauda, 2020, p. 29). However, it is also crucial that students are well connected to their teacher(s). Younger children's relatedness to their teacher has been described as having a "primary influence on their motivation to engage in and value school tasks" (Daniels et al., 2001, p. 254–255).

- M = Me: The degree to which children believe they can complete a task or how well they think they will do on it influences their motivation (Wigfield, 1997). If this seems familiar, it is likely because this dimension of the SMILE acronym aligns with the E component of SEVT (see Chapter 1 for a more detailed explanation of SEVT)—namely, children's expectancies for success. Psychologist *Jacquelynne Eccles* at the University of California, Irvine and her colleagues refined the SEVT motivation model and have conducted many studies supportive of it (for a review see Eccles & Wigfield, 2020).

    Similarly, the life work of renowned Stanford psychologist *Albert Bandura* (e.g., Bandura, 1997), offers substantial support for the role an individual's self-efficacy plays in shaping their motivation. Simply put, students who believe they can successfully complete a given reading task are generally more motivated to participate in that task. Teachers can nurture students' self-efficacy for reading tasks by helping them set achievable goals and by gradually increasing the level of challenge in accordance with students' progress (Barber & Klauda, 2020).

- I = Importance: This dimension of the SMILE acronym is also grounded in SEVT. Recall that, according to SEVT, a young reader might value or prioritize a reading task if they understand it as being useful to them (having utility value) (Eccles, 2005). Teachers can support students in recognizing the relevance of reading tasks by making explicit how completing such tasks helps them reach *their* short-term goals (e.g., building a lego set, caring for a pet, making cupcakes) and *their* long-term goals (e.g., reading a chapter book, reading as well as a sibling, becoming an astronaut).

- L = Liking: This dimension of the SMILE acronym is rooted in SEVT too. According to SEVT, a young reader is more likely to engage deeply in reading and related tasks when they sincerely enjoy doing them (Eccles, 2005). When children associate doing the actual work of reading and/or completing reading tasks with having fun, they are more likely to seek out these experiences and exert the effort required to complete them. It is important to note that the liking to which the SMILE acronym refers does not come from extrinsic (external) rewards (e.g., prizes, praise), but from true intrinsic enjoyment of the task.

  Many extrinsic rewards (e.g., stickers, toys) have been found to work against children's existing interest in reading. However, a seminal study by *Barbara Marinak*, dean of the School of Education at Mount St. Mary's University, and *Linda Gambrell*, professor emerita at Clemson University (2008), did find that rewarding children's reading with books they wanted to read supported their intrinsic reading motivation.

  Another evidence-based way to support students' intrinsic motivation is to offer meaningful choices (Guthrie & Wigfield, 2017). Meaningful choices empower students to make decisions about their own learning. An example of a meaningful choice might be to offer a younger child a choice between two or three classroom pets to research. A second example would be to then offer the same child a choice of several books on the selected pet to begin their research.

- E = Engagement: Task engagement can be described as a symptom of a child's underlying motivation (Unrau & Quirk, 2014). If motivation for a reading task is high, students are more likely to expend the energy necessary to complete the task. Teachers often make judgments about students' underlying motivation based upon their own observations of what they believe to be engaged behaviors (e.g., intense focus) and/or disengaged behaviors (e.g., abandoning a task). Teacher observations are important; however, of equal importance are students' own insights.

Guthrie and Wigfield's SMILE acronym affords an accessible overview of seminal reading motivation findings, many of the influential scholars associated with them, and key motivation and engagement processes. However, the acronym is not intended to be comprehensive. A potentially important oversight related to maximizing reading motivation is the role children's perceived costs may play in influencing their motivation to read and complete related tasks. According to SEVT, the overall value one attributes to a task depends, in part, on what they understand to be the drawback(s) associated with it (Flake et al., 2015).

Larger-scale quantitative studies involving adults (e.g., Perez et al., 2014) have found that anticipated costs can deter them from engaging in various activities. Relatedly, smaller qualitative studies suggest some children may associate costs with their reading intervention participation and that these costs can matter a great deal to them.

- Erickson (2019) found that despite identifying advantages of participation in a school-sponsored summer reading camp, two out of the three second-grade boys studied reported being hesitant to attend future camp reading lessons because they had become disinterested in the books provided there.
- Erickson and colleagues (2020) found that 5 out of 14 kindergarten through second-grade students reported wanting to opt out of their reading intervention program. All students identified advantages of their participation; however, perceived costs (e.g., lack of autonomy; too much challenge) appeared to outweigh benefits for some students.

Like the research discussed in the previous section, the studies introduced here can support you in making clear why it is important to closely examine young children's developing reading motivation. In the early stages of your work, you are encouraged to obtain a full copy of any articles or chapters you think might support your project and add each one to your electronic table. In the final stages, when you are interpreting your findings, you should come back to these studies and/or others you find on your own to make sense of your findings in relation to what others have found.

Together, the research highlighted here indicates a clear need to monitor and support children's motivation for reading and related tasks. For older learners, this may be as simple as inviting them to complete a survey or a feedback questionnaire, and/or conversing with them about what they appreciate and what might be improved in a reading program. Working with younger (K–2) readers can be more challenging. Younger children's less mature development can make it difficult for them to attend, understand, and/or respond to questions posed by adults. However, the literature synthesized next can support you in overcoming these issues.

ELICITING CHILDREN'S PERCEPTIONS

There is no question that tremendous care must be taken when aiming to elicit younger children's perceptions of anything, including their reading programs. Three common concerns specific to kindergarten through second-grade students include the following: (1) difficulty completing paper and pencil research tools (e.g., surveys, questionnaires), (2) less mature capacities for expressive language (compared to older children), and (3) the potential, given imbalanced power dynamics, for young children to offer answers they believe adults want to hear (Measelle et al., 1998).

However, in light of the United Nations Convention on the Rights of the Child (see the introduction to this book for more information), most agree that we should make a sincere effort to elicit children's perceptions of all programs that directly impact them and ethically involve them in the process of generating knowledge about them by conducting research (Arnott & Wall, 2021). Though young children's perceptions of their school reading programs are severely underrepresented in the empirical literature, many researchers across a variety of fields have successfully navigated the three concerns listed above.

Summarized below are a few of these influential studies. They are offered to assist you in supporting the argument that children's motivation-related perceptions can be successfully elicited and to also give you a sense of some of the tools that have been employed to do so. Note that this is certainly not an exhaustive list of methods and that more detailed descriptions of why and how to use specific tools and techniques are offered in Chapter 4. You are again encouraged to collect and organize any studies you think might be helpful in carrying out your own case study project.

- Measelle and colleagues (1998) created and validated the Berkeley Puppet Interview to measure children's achievement motivation among other self-perceptions of school adjustment. The researchers utilized puppets that incorporated children's own speaking styles to assist them in responding more conversationally to the structured interview. This supported the children in comprehending what was being asked of them.

Additionally, children were permitted to offer their responses verbally or nonverbally (e.g., by pointing to a puppet).
- Harris (2015) investigated kindergarten through second-grade children's motivation-related perceptions of common classroom literacy practices. She invited the children to engage in a photo-sorting activity. Children were asked to sort seven photos of common classroom literacy routines four separate times according to the categories of well-being, self-efficacy, utility, and perceived difficulty. The conversational style of the interview and provided props (i.e., photos and sorting jars) supported children in understanding and responding to questions.
- Clark and Moss (2015) created and repeatedly and successfully implemented the Mosaic approach to elicit the perspectives of 3- and 4-year-olds as a means of enhancing school programming. The approach makes use of modes of representation and expression that make sense to children (e.g., drawing, taking photographs, giving tours) for the purposes of supporting children's understanding and communication. However, it also employs these techniques to honor children as the "experts in their own lives," and it supports children's agency by inviting them to take the lead in research activities.

As stated before, great care must be taken when striving to learn about children's perceptions of school programming. Careful planning to assist children in both understanding what is being asked and responding in meaningful ways is imperative. Children's rights to participate or not in all aspects of the research must also be respected. Ensuring children are aware of their right to refuse to participate at any time and their right to know what each aspect of their involvement entails is essential. Several of the techniques just discussed can support children's awareness of both; Chapter 4 further discusses gaining children's assent to participate.

SUMMARY

This chapter outlines the importance of and offers supports for connecting teacher research on reading motivation to established policies and reputable scholarly work on the topic. Connecting your study to local (e.g., district, state) and/or national trends specific to reading motivation can help contextualize your work and provide a strong rationale for it. Grounding your work in the findings of influential motivation scholars can help you narrow the focus of your study, select methods, and interpret findings.

This chapter makes use of Guthrie and Wigfield's (2017) SMILE acronym to organize and synthesize some particularly relevant findings from seminal reading motivation studies. The SMILE acronym represents the following: Sharing (social collaboration and interaction), Me (self-efficacy and expectancies for success), Importance (valuing), Liking (intrinsic enjoyment), and Engagement (active task involvement and effort).

Existing studies that have successfully elicited young children's perceptions can offer a road map for overcoming some of the difficulties inherent to working with kindergarten through second- grade students, in particular. While it can be challenging, it is essential to seek out children's own ideas

Table 3.1. Activity 3

Snowballing Exercise

Figure 3.1. *James Dangora*

Step	Tips	Notes
1. Acquire a copy of Marinak and colleagues' (2015) article, "Me and My Reading Profilee: A tool for assessing early reading motivation." Once you gain access to the full text, check it off in the notes column. Marinak, B. A., Malloy, J. B., Gambrell, L. B., & Mazzoni, S. A. (2015). Me and My Reading Profile: A tool for assessing early reading motivation. *The Reading Teacher, 69*(1), 51–62. https://doi-org.unh.idm.oclc.org/10.1002/trtr.1362	• Use a university, workplace, or public library's research database to find a downloadable PDF file. • Enter the article's full title (surrounded by quotes) for quick retrieval. • Save the article in a folder dedicated to your project's literature review.	Did you save a copy of the full text?

2. Read through the article and highlight anything of relevance to your project. Be on the lookout for references (in-text citations) to others' work that you might be able to use to support your own project.	• For example, if you are interested in listing the ways in which motivation is related to a range of academic outcomes, you might highlight the second sentence in the second paragraph on page 51. • Notice that at the end of that sentence, four studies are cited: "(Cunningham & Stanovich, 1998; Guthrie & Humenick, 2004; Morgan & Fuchs, 2007)."	List the studies you are interested in reviewing here.
3. Now go to the full reference list (at the end of the article) and highlight the studies you intend to review for your project.	• At this stage in the game, it is ok to identify all studies that might be relevant to your work. • Create an electronic table within which you list the study (full citation), the abstract or a summary of key findings, and a category (e.g., academic outcomes related to reading motivation) for sorting.	Did you create a table to organize your literature?
4. Use your university, workplace, and/or public library's research database again to obtain full copies, or at a minimum, the abstracts of the studies you included in your literature table. You might also use Google Scholar to locate these studies. Not all articles are available via Google Scholar; however, this is an efficient and free way to collect abstracts.	• At a minimum, read each study's abstract to decide whether it is a good fit for your project. • Consider downloading and saving complete copies of highly relevant articles for closer review. • Remove any irrelevant studies from your literature table. • Complete the literature table cells for the studies you intend to keep. • Repeat the snowballing process with the new studies as needed.	How many studies remain in your table? Do you need more?

about their motivation. Techniques that may be of help include the use of props, drawing, and giving tours.

REFERENCES

Archambault, I., Eccles, J. S., & Vida, M. N. (2010). Ability self-concepts and subjective value in literacy: Joint trajectories from grades 1–12. *Journal of Educational Psychology, 102*(4), 804–816. https://doi.org/10.1037/a0021075

Arnott, L., & Wall, K. (Eds.). (2021). *Research through play: Participatory methods in early childhood.* SAGE Publications Ltd.

Bandura, A. (1997). *Self-efficacy: The exercise of self control.* W. H. Freeman.

Barber, A. T., & Klauda, S. L. (2020). How reading motivation and engagement enable reading achievement: Policy implications. *Policy Insights from the Behavioral and Brain Sciences, 7*(1), 27–34. https://doi.org/10.1177/2372732219893385

Clark, A., & Moss, P. (2015). *Listening to young children: The Mosaic approach* (2nd ed.). Jessica Kingsley.

Daniels, D. H., Kalkman, D. L., & McCombs, B. L. (2001). Young children's perspectives on learning and teacher practices in different classroom contexts: Implications for motivation. *Early Education and Development, 12*(2), 253–273.

Deci, E. L., & Ryan, R. M. (2002). Self-determination research: Reflections and future directions. In E. L. Deci & R. M. Ryan (Eds.), *Handbook of self-determination research* (pp. 431–441). University of Rochester Press.

Eccles, J. (2005). Subjective task value and the Eccles et al. model of achievement-related choices. In A. J. Elliot & C. S. Dweck (Eds.), *Handbook of competence and motivation* (pp. 105–121). Guilford.

Eccles, J. S., & Wigfield, A. (2020). From expectancy-value theory to situated expectancy-value theory: A developmental, social cognitive, and sociocultural perspective on motivation. *Contemporary Educational Psychology, 61.* https//doi.org/10.1016/j.cedpsych.2020.101859

Erickson, J. D. (2019). Primary readers' perceptions of a camp guided reading intervention: A qualitative case study of motivation and engagement. *Reading & Writing Quarterly, 35*(4), 354–373. https://doi.org/10.1080/10573569.2018.1548952

Erickson, J. D., Condie, C., & Wharton-McDonald, R. (2020). Harnessing the power of young readers' perceptions to support motivation. *The Reading Teacher, 73*(6), 777–787. https://doi.org/10.1002/trtr.1895

Flake, J. K., Barron, K. E., Hulleman, C., McCoach, B. D., & Welsh, M. E. (2015). Measuring cost: The forgotten component of expectancy-value theory. *Contemporary Educational Psychology, 41*, 232–244. https://doi.org/10.1016/j.cedpsych.2015.03.002

Guthrie, J. T., & Wigfield, A. (2017). Literacy engagement and motivation: Rationale, research, teaching, and assessment. In D. Lapp & D. Fisher (Eds.), *Handbook on research on teaching the English language arts* (pp. 57–84). Routledge. https:doi.org/10.4324/9781315650555-3

Harris, P. (2015). "Words and stuff": Exploring children's perspectives of classroom reading in the early school years. *Australian Journal of Language and Literacy, 31*(1), 27–37.

Jacobs, J. E., Lanza, S., Osgood, D. W., Eccles, J. S., & Wigfield, A. (2003). Changes in children's self-competence and values: Gender and domain differences across grades one through twelve. *Child Development, 73*(2), 509–527. https://doi.org/10.1111/1467-8624.00421

Marinak, B. A., & Gambrell, L. B. (2008). Intrinsic motivation and rewards: What sustains young children's engagement with text? *Literacy Research and Instruction, 47*(1), 9–26. https://doi.org/10.1080/19388070701749546

Measelle, J. R., Ablow, J. C., Cowan, P. A., & Cowan, C. P. (1998). Assessing young children's views of their academic, social, and emotional lives: An evaluation of the self-perception scales of the Berkeley Puppet Interview. *Child Development, 69*(6), 1556–1576. https://doi.org/10.1111/j.1467-8624.1998.tb06177.x

Perez, T., Cromley, J. G., & Kaplan, A. (2014). The role of identity development, values, and costs in college STEM retention. *Journal of Educational Psychology, 106*(1), 315–329. https://doi.org/10.1037/a0034027

Sperling, R. A., & Head, D. M. (2002). Reading attitudes and literacy skills in pre-kindergarten and kindergarten children. *Early Childhood Education Journal, 29*(4), 233–236. https://doi.org/10.1023/A:1015129623552

Unrau, N. J., & Quirk, M. (2014). Reading motivation and reading engagement: Clarifying commingled conceptions. *Reading Psychology, 35*(3), 260–284.

Wigfield, A. (1997). Children's motivations for reading and writing engagement. In J. T. Guthrie & A. Wigfield (Eds.), *Reading engagement: Motivating readers through integrated instruction* (pp. 14–33). International Reading Association.

Wigfield, A., Eccles, J. S., Fredricks, J. A., Simpkins, S., Roeser, R. W., & Schiefele, U. (2015). Development of achievement motivation and engagement. In M. E. Lamb & M. Lerner (Eds.), *Handbook of child psychology and developmental science: Socioemotional processes* (7th ed., pp. 657–700). John Wiley & Sons.

Wigfield, A., Eccles, J. S., Yoon, K. S., Harold, R. D., Arbreton, A., Freedman-Doan, K., & Blumenfeld, P. C. (1997). Changes in children's competence beliefs and subjective task values across the elementary school years: A three-year study. *Journal of Educational Psychology, 89*, 451–469.

Chapter 4

Data Collection

Deciding What to Collect and How to Collect It

Joy Dangora Erickson and Beth Fornauf

> "So, you read those words on your computer and then you listen to what I said to you every night?!"—Chrissy, age 6

Chrissy was an especially observant young research partner. She wanted to know exactly what the adults on the research team were doing now and what they would be doing later. She found it fascinating that a member of the team would take the day's recorded conversations home and listen to them again. "Why do you want to listen to them again?" Chrissy asked. The lead researcher explained that she wanted to listen to what Chrissy told the team again so that she could write it down and read it over to make sure she understood what Chrissy was trying to say. Chrissy seemed pleased that her ideas were being taken so seriously.

Listening to children is an important part of gaining insight into their motivation for any school program. Some advise against interviewing young children for fear that an imbalance of power between child and teacher will result in the child sharing only what they believe the teacher wants to hear (Forster & Eperjesi, 2021). Although this is possible, many studies (e.g., Erickson, 2019a, 2019b) have found ways to mitigate the imbalance of power and have yielded insights from children's interview responses that otherwise likely would have gone unnoticed.

Participatory research methods, for example, involve children making decisions about and/or leading aspects of the research process (Clark &

Moss, 2011). A participatory method described in greater detail later in this chapter is that of student-led walking tours. Though an adult may initially frame a walking-tour interview with an opening question or two, the child quickly assumes the lead by taking the adult on a tour of one or more spaces related to the adult-posed question(s). When comfortable leading the tour, many children open up about their experiences and are excited to share their understandings and opinions.

Another way to help children feel comfortable answering questions about their reading program is by involving a trusted adult in the interviewing process. For some children, this may be a student teacher or a school counselor. For others it may be an older sibling or a guardian. University or college researchers have also served as trusted interviewers for children (after spending time building rapport with them). Enlisting a trusted adult who is not directly responsible for delivering the child's reading instruction can enhance the trustworthiness of findings.

Children's views are crucial for understanding their motivation for school reading programs and, in turn, for supporting their developing motivation. It is worth investing the time and effort necessary to elicit children's own perspectives. However, converging pieces of evidence are also needed to reach trustworthy conclusions. One interview, no matter how substantive, is typically not enough to support claims about a child's motivation.

Instead, you should look for confirming and disconfirming evidence from multiple sources. This is called *triangulation* (Creswell & Poth, 2018). By highlighting the ways more than one source and/or type of data offered a similar finding, you are bolstering the *trustworthiness* of your findings or the likelihood that your findings are consistent with the data collected (Merriam & Tisdell, 2016). Sources of evidence you might consider in addition to student interviews include your own observations, the perspectives of guardians, and/or students' work samples.

This chapter introduces you to several types of data—namely, *observations*, *artifacts,* and *interviews*—and invites you to consider which specific pieces of data might best support the answering of your research question. Multiple forms of the three types of data have been successfully employed to examine young children's motivation for school reading programs. It will help to have the latest iteration of your research question nearby as you work through the remainder of this chapter.

THREE GENERAL TYPES OF DATA

Observations

Researchers use observations to note the activities taking place at a research site (e.g., classroom, intervention group), as well as the behaviors of individuals at the site (Creswell & Poth, 2018). Observations are commonly included in case study projects, including those centering on children's motivation. For practicing teachers, observations often take the form of *field notes* written on the spot, or of *reflective diary/journal entries* written shortly after an observation.

One advantage of taking field notes is being able to document children's comments and actions in the moment rather than trying to recall them later (Dana & Yendol-Hoppey, 2020). Because of this, field notes do not typically include interpretation but, rather, describe the events, dialogue, or activities being observed. An excerpt from field notes generated during a case study exploring two English learners' (ELs) motivation for their reading intervention program appears in Textbox 4.1.

Reflective diary/journal entries, on the other hand, allow time to think through that which just occurred. This can be helpful in processing what you observed and in identifying where to go next. An example of a reflective journal entry written shortly after closely observing one specific child in the EL motivation case study during intervention is offered in Textbox 4.2. The entry sparked the researcher to follow up with the child about missing her classmate in a later interview.

It can be advantageous to take field notes and to reflect in a diary/journal; however, it can also be time consuming. Either of these methods, in combination with additional data collected in other ways, may be enough to answer your research question. Using a tablet to take field notes or reflect on observations can be more time efficient in the moment and again later when you analyze your data. Additionally, or alternatively, if working with a team, another member of the team can take field notes while you teach. University researchers, administrators, and/or instructional coaches may be willing to observe and document students' engagement in your reading lessons.

Regardless of whether you decide to take field notes, reflect in a diary/journal, or do both, what children say and do during observations can be compared to what they share in interviews. Adult observations of children's engagement complement children's self-reports of their motivation by offering another source of data that can support and/or challenge children's own perceptions. To make and support claims you must look for and identify clear patterns in your data.

TEXTBOX 4.1: SAMPLE FIELD NOTE EXCERPT

Date: 4/15/2021
Time: 8:30 a.m.–8:45 a.m.
Location: Reading Intervention Room
Intervention: Scott Foresman Early Reading Intervention (ERI)
Observee(s): Lil & Gemma (Kindergarten students)
Observer: Joy D. Erickson (Researcher)

Initial Impressions of Engagement:

Both girls entered the intervention space with energy and focus. They were actively involved in the letter, keyword, sound drill. Engagement suffered during round robin reading. Specifically, both girls struggled to attend while their peers were reading. Off-task behaviors included staring at the wall, slouching in one's seat, and fidgeting with intervention materials.

As I entered the intervention space, I asked both Lil and Gemma if it was OK that (1) I was there watching what they were doing during the ERI session and (2) I took notes about what I saw. I explained that I needed to take notes to remember what I saw. Both girls granted me permission to do these things.

Interventionist reviews letter, keyword, sound drill with the group. She models how to do the drill with two letters (S, K) before asking the kids to join in.

Lil and Gemma appear to eagerly participate. Both are focused and complete all 16 letters, accurately offering each keyword and pronouncing the sound associated with each letter.

Interventionist praises their good work. Gemma smiles. The interventionist asks the group to take out their journals. Both girls quickly comply.

Gemma plays with a paper towel (serves as an eraser for dry erase board work) while she waits for other students to take out their journals. Lil pages through her journal.

The interventionist changes her mind and instead asks the kids to take out the ERI book *Bud the Pup*. Again, Lil and Gemma do this quickly.

The interventionist asks the group to identify and explain various parts of the book (e.g., cover, title page). Both girls raise their hands to respond to questions and respond eagerly and accurately when called upon. They appear mostly engaged.

The interventionist asks each member of the group (five students total) to each take turns reading aloud a page from the book.

Engagement appears to break down as the girls wait for their turn to read. Lil slumps in her seat and does not follow along as another group member reads. She appears to be frowning at the wall. The interventionist attempts to direct her back to the text: "Lil, your finger needs to be on the page following along." Lil complies initially, but her eyes begin to wander around the room again as she waits for her turn. Again, the interventionist redirects her: "Lil, we're turning the page now."

Both girls are asked to sit up and "touch" the words as they are read by others. Both girls struggle to follow along. Gemma also looks around the room as other group members read rather laboriously.

Lil gets the chance to read her page and does so easily: "Diz said, 'Run, Bud!'" She reads accurately and with expression.

It's Gemma's turn next, and she struggles to read what's on the page. The interventionist coaches her through the sentence. Lil slouches in her seat again and looks at a poster to her right.

Gemma also begins to drift as other group members read a page for the second time.

Lil begins playing with the materials in her reading folder and several items drop to the ground. She retrieves them. The interventionist again asks her to follow along.

The final page is read, and the kids are asked to pack up and line up at the door. Both girls do this quickly and exit.

When multiple sources (e.g., student, teacher, instructional coach) and/or types of data (e.g., student interview, field notes, reflective diary/journal) converge to suggest, for example, that a student displays sustained on-task behavior when reading a particular genre or series, you can feel confident claiming that that particular aspect of your reading program supports the child's motivation to read within it.

Before conducting any observations pay attention to these five important guidelines adapted from the work of Hancock and Algozzine (2011):

- Be sure to first decide what you need to observe to answer your research question. For example, if you are interested in knowing more about a student's engagement in their reading group (as an indicator of their motivation for the group), you might decide to reflect daily in a diary

TEXTBOX 4.2: SAMPLE REFLECTIVE JOURNAL ENTRY

Joy D. Erickson
5/5/2021

Gemma and Lil's ERI Session (9:00 a.m.–9:30 a.m.)

During this virtual observation, I noticed that both Gemma and Lil more actively participated in particular aspects of their reading intervention. Overall, Lil was quicker to comply with her interventionist's requests. Specifically, she got materials out immediately when asked and almost always raised her hand to answer questions. Gemma also complied with most requests, but it took her a bit more time and she occasionally needed directions repeated.

Gemma appeared to enter the room more enthusiastically than Lil. She immediately began telling the interventionist about her weekend. Lil remarked to Gemma that she wished their other friend, Linn, who remained in the classroom, was with them. Lil looked a bit down as she took her seat.

When I interview Lil next week, I will ask her more about this. Specifically, I am wondering if Lil regularly misses Linn during ERI lessons and, if she does, might that sense of loss be influencing her motivation for the program? Might occasionally inviting Linn to join Lil better support Lil's motivation for the program? Though I will not directly ask these questions as not to influence Lil's answers, I will look to see if Lil mentions Linn in our interview on her own. If she does not, I might ask her who Linn is and why she told Gemma that she wished Linn could come with them to intervention.

Both girls perked up for the letter, keyword, sound drill. They seemed to like how the interventionist sped up the drill as they went on. Though Gemma struggled more than Lil (which is typical), she appeared to maintain her level of enthusiasm for the drill, smiling often. Gemma also persisted until the end.

When the interventionist asked the girls to get out their ERI books, they both did so in a timely manner. Lil had her book out and ready first. The interventionist announced that each member of the group (five children) would read a page aloud. Lil sighed at this request; it appeared as though she was not excited to participate in this task. Both

> girls became distracted while the other students in the group were reading and needed to be reminded when it was their turn. When I interview Lil next week, I will ask her specifically how she feels about the round robin approach to reading used today. I am wondering if her sigh was a signal of her feelings about this aspect of the intervention.

on what you perceive to be the student's on-task (e.g., focused attention, task completion) and/or off-task (e.g., inattention, incomplete task) behaviors and/or take field notes one or more times per week for several weeks. In either case, you should identify and clearly define the behaviors you observe.
- Create an observation guide (template) to support your taking of field notes and/or diary reflections (see Textboxes 4.1 and 4.2 for examples). At a minimum, your template should include spaces to note the date, time, location, name of individual(s) being observed, name/description of reading program, and your initial impression(s) of what you intended to observe (e.g., child's level of engagement).
- Gain access to your participants' authentic behaviors as best you can in part by developing trusting relationships. Though many teachers typically develop trusting relationships with students and organically function as the leader of classroom activities, care should be taken to blend research activities as naturally into classroom routines as possible and alleviate any suspicions children may have about the research process by disclosing procedures and answering questions honestly in developmentally appropriate ways.
- Recognize and mitigate (as best you can) any biases that could impact your observations. Biases come in all shapes and sizes; identifying them is key to limiting their influence. Past experiences and/or current feelings about your job, a program, a child, and/or a family, among other things, can color your observations and bias your findings. Though it is impossible to free your study entirely of bias, you should try your best to minimize it. It is helpful to make a list of any feelings or views that could interfere with your observations and ask a trusted colleague to assist you in regularly reviewing your work for bias.
- Uphold all ethical and legal requirements for observing children. Though you may not need legal permission to reflect in a diary/journal about your students' behaviors, ethically, it makes good sense to disclose your method to the students involved and their guardians and to gain both groups' permission to do so. A child-friendly description (pictures can help) of what you plan to do and why, is often sufficient. Additionally,

students are entitled to complete anonymity and confidentiality; assigning each participating child a pseudonym from the start can ensure their identities are protected.

Artifacts

Recall that to answer your research question you should collect several relevant types of data from several sources to identify patterns. It is from these patterns that you will make and support claims about a student's or students' motivation for a reading program and make changes intended to better support their motivation. Student work is one type of artifact that can support you in this goal. Though there are infinite examples of student work products that might be relevant to your inquiry, *students' journal entries* can be especially helpful in offering insight into their motivation for a program.

Many teachers invite and support young students in completing journal entries. These entries often include pictures, words, or a combination of both. Do not attempt to independently make meaning from children's drawings; there is too much potential for misinterpretations. Instead, invite children to explain their drawings to you and scribe their responses. Figure 4.1 depicts journal entries created by kindergarten and first-grade students, respectively.

The *Me and My Reading Profile* (MMRP) (Marinak et al., 2015) survey of reading motivation is another artifact that may support your inquiry. Recall that you were asked to acquire the journal article (featured in *The Reading Teacher*) that includes this survey in Chapter 3's snowballing exercise (Activity 3). The MMRP has been shown to be a valid and reliable way to

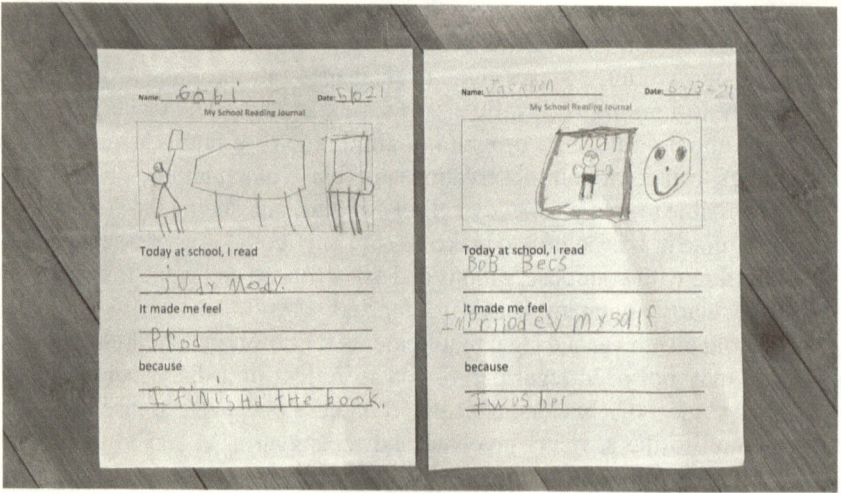

Figure 4.1. Sample Kindergarten Reading Journal Entries. *Created by chapter author's*

Figure 4.2. Child Completing MMRP Survey. *Created by chapter author's child*

measure the motivation of kindergarten, first-, and second-grade students. Figure 4.2 shows a kindergarten child completing the MMRP individually; her teacher reads the prompts aloud to her.

The MMRP consists of 20 items that measure children's general self-concept as a reader (i.e., the degree to which they believe they are competent at reading), their valuing of reading, and a construct the authors refer to as "literacy out loud," which pertains to how children feel when reading out loud. The MMRP can be administered to students individually or in a group setting. Be sure to carefully review (and consider practicing) the complete administration guidelines included in the journal article before giving this survey.

MMRP results may be used to support or challenge information gleaned from other data sources (e.g., student interviews, field notes). For example, if a child reports in an interview and/or writes in their journal that they do not like attending their reading group or reading intervention because they do not like to read, you would expect to see their general dislike of reading show up on the MMRP. Multiple MMRP questions probe children's liking of reading. If the child reports consistently on the survey that they enjoy reading, a follow-up interview is warranted to better understand the discrepancy.

The MMRP can also be used to gauge whether and to what extent children's general motivation changed from the beginning to the end of your inquiry. Though you will not be able to say for sure whether the specific reading program included in your study impacted child participants' motivation to read, if positive or neutral, results can be used (in conjunction with other data) to support some claims (e.g., it does not appear that the reading program(s) is/are hindering this/these child's/children's more general motivation to read).

Alternatively, in the case where a child's or group's motivation appears to have declined over the inquiry period, you might look for similar patterns across collected data. Do field notes, journal entries, and/or interviews suggest children's attitude(s) toward reading within and/or outside of the program have become more negative? If so, you might set a goal with the children to improve their reading attitude(s) and make changes to the reading program to support this goal. Chapter 8 explains in detail how to analyze and interpret quantitative (i.e., numerical) data from the MMRP.

Interviews

Interviews can offer much insight into how children perceive their reading program(s). In many instances, researchers have gleaned information from children they likely otherwise would not have uncovered. When conducting interviews with younger children, it is important to employ methods that make good sense to them. Interview methods should incorporate children's own values, interests, experiences, and modes of communication, while affording them some control over the interview process (O'Reilly & Dogra, 2017).

In some cases, it may be appropriate for the teacher who facilitates the reading program to lead the interview; if a teacher regularly confers with students and they are accustomed to being questioned and offering honest feedback about the program this may be a good option. In other cases, interviewing your own students might not be the best choice. Remember that many young children aim to please; you might not get the most accurate or helpful information interviewing your own students. Another trusted adult (e.g., classroom assistant, school counselor) or sometimes an older sibling or relative can be a better choice.

Additionally, it is a good idea to conduct more than one interview with each child of interest. For example, you might elect to interview a child participant one time per week for three weeks. Doing so can support you in recognizing patterns in your data and in making well-justified claims and instructional decisions. Below are two participatory interview techniques that have been used successfully to probe kindergarten through second-grade students' program-specific reading motivation.

CONVERSATIONAL DRAWING INTERVIEWS

A conversational drawing interview can be an excellent first interview approach for young children who have limited experiences with adult-led interviews. The drawing component serves as a mode of communication many are familiar with and offers children something active to do while conversing with the interviewer. Typically, the interviewer begins by inviting the child to participate in the drawing interview (i.e., requests assent) explaining in child-friendly language what the pair will do and why. For example, you might say something like:

> Hi Lil. How are you today? I was wondering if you might want to draw and talk about how you do reading with Mrs. Bien for a little bit with me. I'm trying to learn more about how kids do reading at school and what they like and don't like. Is that something you might want to talk with me about? I will ask you to draw a picture of how you do reading with Mrs. Bien, and then I will ask you some questions about what you really like and what you might not like as much about your reading time. I will also record our conversation so that I can remember what we talked about. Is that OK?

If the child grants assent, the pair would move to a more private location provisioned with drawing supplies. Consider permitting the child to choose the location or choose from a set of pre-selected options to increase their control in the process. Many researchers elect to also allow the interviewee to control the recording device (with adult assistance).

Once settled the child should be presented with a variety of art materials (e.g., colored pencils, markers, crayons) and again invited to draw how they do reading specific to the reading program of interest. It can be helpful to allow the child several minutes to get started before asking any questions. At that point clarifying questions can be helpful to understand what the child is drawing. For example, if you notice a figure in the drawing you might ask, "Is that you?" and follow up with "What are you doing there?"

A stream of conversational questions is likely to follow these initial clarifying remarks. Once the conversation seems comfortable for the child you might begin asking questions more aligned with your study's aims. For example, if you are interested in better understanding what the child appreciates and/or does not appreciate about the program, you might ask them whether they enjoy doing that which they have illustrated in their drawing. Examples of questions that might be helpful include the following:

- Do you like reading the book/doing that activity that you drew there? Why or why not?

- Do you like working with the people you have included in your drawing? Why or why not?
- What else do you do during this time? How do you feel about that/those things? Why?
- It seems that you are playing a reading game here. Is that right? Is it fun for you? Why?

You will notice that each of the above questions is followed by a "why?" question; it is important to document children's rationales for their preferences whenever possible. These rationales can support you in deciding whether and how to modify reading program routines. You should end the interview immediately if the child offers any indication that they no longer want to participate. Otherwise, end the interview when it feels appropriate to do so. Most children enjoy this experience, and it may be necessary to end the interview before the child has lost interest in the activity to resume other classroom activities.

Be sure to thank the child for teaching you about how they do reading. Many children like to keep their drawings. Though you will analyze the child's words and not the drawing per se, you will want to have a record of it to refer to when reviewing the interview transcript. For this reason, be sure to take a picture of the drawing and store it confidentially in a secure and organized location before permitting the child to take it.

Walking-Tour Interviews

Student-led walking-tour interviews are another participatory interview approach that can be used to elicit children's motivation-related perceptions of reading programs (e.g., Erickson, 2019a, 2019b). Grounded in Clark and Moss's (2011) "tour" method, children are invited to lead adults on a tour of the learning space(s) associated with the specific reading program of focus. It is within the reading space that children show, manipulate, and discuss the tools (e.g., books, white boards, letter tiles, anchor charts) they use to do reading there and report on their feelings about those tools.

Again, in many cases another trusted adult (e.g., school counselor, student teacher, older sibling) who is not the facilitator of the reading program may be best positioned to accompany the child on the interview. Walking-tour interviews aimed at examining children's motivation for a reading program and the rationale(s) behind their self-reported motivation might begin outside the child's classroom.

There, the adult (after gaining assent from the child and inviting them to start the recording device) might pose the question: "If you could choose whether to go to [place where reading program usually occurs] to do reading as you usually do or go to [another place where the child does some form of reading], which would you choose?" The adult should follow up by asking for the child's rationale for their stated choice (i.e., "Why would you choose to go there?").

If the child chooses the reading program/setting that is the focus of your case study, the adult participating in the interview should ask the child if they would be willing to take the adult to the space, show them around, and explain what they enjoy about doing reading there. If the child refuses to choose (kids do on occasion resist a binary response), for the sake of time, the adult might ask them if they would be willing to tour the space most relevant to your case study. If the child chooses the reading space that is not the focus of your study, they might give a tour of the preferred space first followed by the space of interest.

When touring the space of interest, the interviewer should take care to ask as many questions as needed to adequately address the research question(s). If primarily interested in the child's motivation for doing reading in the space/program the interviewer might ask:

- Tell me more about why you said you would rather do reading here?
- What do you like/dislike about doing reading here?
- Do you think other people like doing reading here? Why?
- Can you show me the things you use to do reading here? How do you feel about this/these [books, journals, letter tiles, etc.] you're showing me? Why do you feel that way?
- Is there anything you would change about doing reading here to make it more fun?

It is within these walking-tour-style interviews that children tend to reveal the most about their program-specific likes and dislikes. Therefore, these interviews tend to take longer to complete than conversational drawing interviews.

If using both approaches, it can be useful to conduct conversational drawing interviews a week or two before walking tours. This way you will already have a sense of children's motivation for the program and can ask any clarifying and/or more nuanced questions you may have. For example, if a child reveals in a drawing interview that they do not like a particular text or series used in the reading program, the interviewer can use the walking-tour interview to confirm this view and to ask the child to show them the specific features of the text they understand to be problematic. Be sure to thank children for their time at the end of the interview.

A SAMPLE DESIGN PLAN

Recall that taking care to include several types of data from multiple sources is important for triangulating data, and triangulating data is necessary to reach trustworthy conclusions. Therefore, you want to try and select data that facilitates the triangulation process. Let us say that your research aim is to examine a group of children's motivation for their small group reading program. Specifically, we are aiming to collect data that will allow us to answer the cluster of related research questions first presented in Chapter 2:

- *"What does this group of children understand to be the advantages and/ or disadvantages of participating in their small group reading lessons?"*
- *"If permitted to choose, would these children attend their small group reading lessons? Why or why not?"*

First, we must consider whom we will consult to answer our research questions. The consideration of three knowledgeable people is probably enough to reach trustworthy conclusions. We will most definitely want to consider the children's own views. The reading teacher's views are also arguably highly relevant. A third, more neutral observer (e.g., researcher, building principal, instructional coach) can be a good source of comparative data.

Specific to the children, we should conduct at least two interviews. We might first elect to conduct (or employ someone else to conduct) a drawing interview with each child after several weeks of observing the reading program. This interview might be followed up a week or so later with a walking-tour interview. During this approximately three-week time period, we might also collect three reading journal entries (one per week) from each child. These children's perceived advantages and disadvantages, as well as their willingness to attend the program, should be able to be captured using the interview methods and journal entries previously discussed.

The reading teacher might begin taking field notes and/or focusing their reflective journal entries on the children's engagement during reading sessions. The reading teacher might start doing this a week or so before drawing interviews occur and continue for several weeks thereafter. Their notes can then be compared to what the children report during interviews and in their journal entries. Put differently, evidence in teacher observations should be carefully reviewed to determine whether it supports or undermines students' own views.

Let us suppose that the building principal is willing to offer a third perspective on the children's motivation. The principal might attend as many of the children's small group reading lessons as necessary over the month-and-a-half-long project duration to get a sense of each child's willingness to participate in small group reading sessions. The principal would take detailed field notes during observations that could be compared to both the children's and the teacher's reports.

It is easy to collect too much data and feel overwhelmed. That is why it is important to choose the data you will collect carefully. You should strive to collect the data you believe is most likely to support you in answering your research questions.

SUMMARY

This chapter introduced several important sources of data that can help you answer your research questions. Children's insights offer a crucial perspective, but care must be taken when involving them in the research process. Allowing children the opportunity to be partners in the research process, through a variety of methods, can lead to key insights about their learning. A willingness to invite and foreground children's perspectives, in conjunction with additional evidence from trusted adults, allows you to triangulate your data and reach more trustworthy conclusions in your research.

The types of data introduced in this chapter take many forms and serve a variety of purposes. For example, field notes and reflective journals are observation tools that capture events in the moment and/or allow you to reflect on them later. Artifacts such as student work samples or survey results can clarify students' experiences and illuminate discrepancies. Interviews can offer students opportunities to serve as an expert in the research process when they explain their drawings or give tours of learning spaces. Collecting multiple types of data can offer a robust corpus of evidence to answer your research questions.

Keep in mind there is a delicate balance between collecting data and becoming overwhelmed by it. Be purposeful in how and from whom you collect data, while also taking care to acquire diverse perspectives through a range of techniques. Focusing on your research questions will help you make informed decisions about data collection. As you build a plan for design, consider which individuals can offer complementary insights, and which types of data are more likely to shed light on your specific area of interest.

Table 4.1. Activity 4

Data Selection Exercise

Figure 4.3. Sample Kindergarten Reading Journal Entries. *Created by James Dangora*

1. Write your research question(s) here:

Highlight the specific aspects of the child participant's/participants' motivation you are interested in learning more about (e.g., perceived advantages and disadvantages of program participation; willingness to participate in the reading program; liking of reading in general)

2. Will you include the student's/students' own perspective(s)?

YES	NO
List the type(s) of data you will collect from the student(s) to answer your research question:	Explain why you have decided not to include the student's/students' own views:
Explain why you have decided to include these specific types of data:	
Note potential opportunities for triangulation:	

3. Will you include the reading teacher's perspective?

YES	NO
List the type(s) of data you will collect from the reading teacher:	Explain why you have decided not to include the teacher's views:
Note potential opportunities for triangulation:	

4. Will you include the perspective(s) of anyone else?

YES	NO
Explain why you will include this person's/these people's perspective(s):	Explain why you have decided not to include any other perspectives:
List the type(s) of data you will collect from this person/these people:	
Note potential opportunities for triangulation:	

REFERENCES

Clark, A., & Moss, P. (2011). *Listening to young children: The Mosaic approach* (2nd ed.). Jessica Kingsley.

Creswell, J. W., & Poth, C. N. (2018). *Qualitative inquiry and research design: Choosing among five approaches.* (4th ed.). Sage.

Dana, N. F., & Yendol-Hoppey, D. (2020). *The reflective educator's guide to classroom research: Learning to teach and teaching to learn through practitioner inquiry* (4th ed.). Corwin.

Erickson, J. D. (2019a). Primary readers' perceptions of a camp guided reading intervention: A qualitative case study of motivation and engagement. *Reading & Writing Quarterly: Overcoming Learning Difficulties, 35*(4), 354–373.

Erickson, J. D. (2019b). Primary students' emic views of reading intervention: A qualitative case study of motivation. *Literacy Research: Theory, Method, and Practice, 68*(1), 86–107.

Forster, C., & Eperjesi, R. (2021). *Action research for student teachers* (2nd ed.). Sage.

Hancock, D. R., & Algozzine, B. (2011). *Doing case study research: A practical guide for beginning researchers* (2nd ed.). Teachers College Press.

Marinak, B. A., Malloy, J. B., Gambrell, L. B., & Mazzoni, S. A. (2015). Me and my reading profile: A tool for assessing early reading motivation. *The Reading Teacher, 69*(1), 51–62. https://doi.org/10.1002/trtr.1362

Merriam, S. B., & Tisdell, E. J. (2016). *Qualitative research: A guide to design and implementation* (4th ed.). Jossey-Bass.

O'Reilly, M., & Dogra, N. (2017). *Interviewing children and young people for research.* Sage.

Chapter 5

How Am I Going to Fit Data Collection into My Packed Day?

Outlining a Data Collection Plan

Joy Dangora Erickson and Kyleigh P. Rousseau

"Are you going to record us today?!"—Izzy, age 5

Izzy loved playing an active role in classroom research. She enjoyed being positioned as an expert during interviews, and she loved when her reading lessons were video recorded. Izzy's teacher and/or another member of the research team would occasionally record Izzy's intervention sessions (with parental consent and child assent) so that they could look back as needed and precisely quote language summarized in journal entries and/or field notes. You may not have time to collect and analyze large amounts of video data; however, it can be helpful to have a few recordings available in case your jottings leave you wondering about specifics.

Izzy's teacher recorded sessions on her iPadpad and saved them in a specific project folder. Though this may seem fairly simple, you might be wondering how you are going to fit particular aspects of the research process into your day. The remainder of this chapter is dedicated to assisting you in identifying opportunities to collect data in your existing daily routines. In truth, "meaningful teacher inquiry should not depart from the daily work of classroom teachers but instead should become a part of their daily work" (Dana & Yendol-Hoppey, 2020, p. 99).

Specifically, the daily morning schedule of kindergarten teacher Mrs. Rousseau will be considered in conjunction with her inquiry questions; a variety of opportunities for data collection will be identified and discussed in the sections that follow. Mrs. Rousseau is interested in knowing more about several students' motivation for her literacy block. This is the first year the children have participated in a formal 90-minute literacy block. Despite giving the children several months to settle into the new routine, Mrs. Rousseau has noticed that a few children remain reluctant to participate.

Having reviewed the scholarly literature, Mrs. Rousseau knows that it is not uncommon for children's motivation to decline as they progress through elementary school. She also knows that children's early experiences matter when it comes to reading motivation. She is wondering if there is something she can do to better support the students' motivation. She grounds her case study in the following questions:

1. "What do these children understand to be the advantages and/or disadvantages of participating in their daily literacy block?"
2. "If permitted to choose, would they participate in it? Why or why not?"
3. "How might the literacy block be shaping their overall motivation to read?"

To answer these questions Mrs. Rousseau will gather the pieces of data in the following bulleted list over the course of a month. It can be difficult to decide how long to collect data. Sometimes the reading program itself dictates the length of a study. For example, if a group of students are participating in a brief (e.g., six-week) summer reading intervention, you might collect data throughout the intervention to inform future interventions for these students or others.

However, in a case like Mrs. Rousseau's where she hopes to gain information that can be used to improve instruction within a longer program, you will want to select a period of time that allows you to collect enough data to make sound changes to ongoing instruction. Mrs. Rousseau has allotted herself a month so that she might balance having adequate time to collect data with being able to respond efficiently to children's motivation needs; the case study is intended to inform and improve instruction that will take place in the near future.

Note that the source of the data (i.e., who is offering the information) is specified after each type listed below; this allows Mrs. Rousseau to be sure data is coming from multiple sources (i.e., perspectives). Recall that gathering multiple types of data from multiple sources supports the process of triangulation (see Chapter 4 for more information on triangulation), which can strengthen conclusions (Creswell & Poth, 2018; Dana & Yendol-Hoppey, 2020). Additionally, the specific question(s) to which each piece of data mainly relates is listed; specifying this affords you another opportunity to check the relevance of your data.

- Daily reflective journal entries (Weeks 1, 2, 3, 4) (Source = Mrs. Rousseau; Research Questions 1, 2, 3)
- Pre (Week 1) and Post (Week 4) *Me and My Reading Profile* (Marinak et al., 2015) survey scores (Source = the children; Research Question 3)
- 20-minute drawing interview (Weeks 1, 2) (Source = the children; Research Questions 1, 3)
- 20-minute walking-tour interview (Weeks 3, 4) (Source = the children; Research Questions 1, 2, 3)
- Field notes (Weeks 1, 2, 3, 4) (Source = Mrs. Rousseau's co-teacher; Research Questions 1, 3)

Having offered a strong rationale for conducting her study, developed clear questions to guide it, and identified the data she will collect to answer those questions, Mrs. Rousseau is ready to begin planning for data collection. Though literacy instruction and practice are woven throughout the kindergarten day, direct instruction primarily takes place in the morning during the literacy block. A typical morning in Mrs. Rousseau's class consists of the following components:

8:30–9:00 = Morning Meeting
9:00–10:30 = Literacy Block (i.e., 10 minutes of phonemic awareness instruction, 20 minutes of phonics instruction, 60 minutes of reading workshop activities that include writing)
10:30–10:50 = Recess
10:50–11:05 = Read Aloud
11:05–11:30 = Lunch

Mrs. Rousseau considers when she might collect each type of data she has identified.

DAILY REFLECTIVE JOURNAL ENTRIES

Mrs. Rousseau will reflect in her journal at least three times a week for each of the study's four weeks. It is ideal to reflect immediately after an observation; however, teachers often do not have this luxury. Mrs. Rousseau is fortunate to have recess after her 90-minute literacy block. Typically, she and her co-teacher take turns going out to recess; she could ask her co-teacher to cover three days a week for the month. On the days she does not do duty, Mrs.

Rousseau plans or sets up for instruction. She could instead use this time to write her reflections. This may result in her having to come in earlier or stay later to make up the planning time.

Alternatively, Mrs. Rousseau could wait until lunchtime, or even after dismissal, to complete her reflections. Either option might be feasible; however, the longer she waits, the greater the chance she might forget important details from the observation.

PRE- AND POST-READING MOTIVATION SURVEYS

Though she recognizes many things could be influencing her students' more general motivation to read, Mrs. Rousseau is curious to know whether each student's motivation to read has changed over the course of her study (1 month). For this reason, she intends to administer the MMRP (see Chapter 4 for information about the MMRP) on the first day and last day of the study. She must read the directions and prompts aloud to her students; this can be done individually or in a group setting. Mrs. Rousseau intends to give the survey to all of her students.

She could do this at the start of the day during morning meeting time. During this time the students are familiar with the routine of being seated in a circle on the carpet with Mrs. Rousseau and/or her co-teacher leading activities. Mrs. Rousseau would have 30 minutes to support the children in completing the MMRP. This might be an excellent time to take the survey.

Alternatively, Mrs. Rousseau could ask students to complete the survey during the reading workshop portion of the literacy block. She could connect the survey to what the students were doing in the literacy block by having a discussion (after they take the survey) about whether the children enjoy the books they have been reading in the literacy block. This could be an especially meaningful workshop session. It appears that Mrs. Rousseau has two viable options for administering the MMRP.

DRAWING INTERVIEW

Drawing interviews are usually conducted one on one (i.e., interviewer and interviewee) and, including setup and cleanup, take about 30 minutes to complete. During the interview, the child participant is invited to draw what they do during the literacy block and explain how they feel about each component. A trusted adult is usually employed to conduct the interview in an effort to elicit honest responses.

Mrs. Rousseau has decided to involve the children's guardians in the interview process when possible. Specifically, for each child she has identified and invited a trusted guardian to come in and conduct the drawing interview. Interviews will take place out of earshot (e.g., in the hallway outside the classroom) to ensure each student's privacy. If a trusted guardian is not able to participate, graciously the school counselor has offered to step in. Assuming the children and their guardians grant permission, the interviews will be audio recorded for transcription.

Mrs. Rousseau would like the children and their guardians to select a time during the first or second week of the study to complete the drawing interview. She intends to send home a calendar that includes the 10 school days with several possible times for each day. Specifically, she will offer 30 minutes before the start of school, recess time, lunchtime, and 30 minutes after school. Previous experience tells Mrs. Rousseau that many children enjoy completing such activities with their loved ones over lunch or snack and that some guardians are only available before or after school. She will ask guardians to select three times and then assign them one of their selected times.

WALKING-TOUR INTERVIEW

Walking-tour interviews are also usually conducted one on one (i.e., interviewer and interviewee) and take about 30 minutes from start to finish to complete. During the interview, the child is invited to take the interviewer on a tour of the space within which their literacy instruction occurs. A trusted adult is again employed to conduct the interview. If a guardian is not able to participate, the school counselor will conduct the interview. Interviews will be audio recorded and transcribed provided permission is granted by the child and guardian(s).

Walking-tour interviews require the literacy space to be largely vacant. To accommodate this requirement, Mrs. Rousseau will invite children and their guardians to select a time when the classroom is empty. She will again send home a calendar that includes available Week 3 and 4 dates and times. She intends to offer 30 minutes before the start of school and 30 minutes after school. Though she prefers that interviews not be conducted during recess for a myriad of reasons, she will note that recess time will be available as needed. Mrs. Rousseau will ask guardians to select three times and then assign them one of their selected times.

FIELD NOTES

Using a template Mrs. Rousseau has provided (for an example see Textbox 4.1 in Chapter 4), her co-teacher will take field notes two or three times per week throughout the month-long study. Mrs. Rousseau's co-teacher will focus on observing how one or two specific children engage in the literacy block each time. This approach should yield at least three close observations for each child involved in the study. Alternatively, Mrs. Rousseau could ask another adult familiar with the children, literacy block, and study to take field notes. A literacy coach, school counselor, or principal might be able to support this work.

STAYING ORGANIZED AND KNOWING WHEN YOU HAVE COLLECTED ENOUGH INFORMATION

As teachers prepare to examine their students' motivation, it is important that they plan their days with intentionality. Kuh and Ponte (2017) describe an intention as "an aim or a plan that guides action in the classroom" (p. 10). These goal-minded plans can support teachers in carrying out their daily work with children in an efficient manner. There are a variety of ways teachers can plan with intentionality to make room for data collection.

A few strategies that support Mrs. Rousseau in this process are grouping like-tasks (e.g., answering/sending e-mails, planning lessons, organizing notes/data), creating weekly to-do lists with the items organized into three time chunks each day (before school, during school, after school), and limiting the length of her chats with other professionals during planning time (Powell, 2009). When grouping like-tasks, it is important to think about all the items on your weekly to-do list. Once you have a list of all the tasks that need to be accomplished for the week, you can then group like-tasks together and schedule a time within your week (e.g., Tuesday before school) to complete them.

Prescheduling your time for the work week can increase work productivity without working longer hours. Mrs. Rousseau's commitment to intentional planning permits her to integrate aspects of the research process, including data collection, into her regular day without adding too many additional hours of work. Mrs. Rousseau is not necessarily working harder, but she is working more efficiently.

Organizing Your Data

It is imperative that you stay highly organized throughout the data collection process. It is extremely frustrating to not be able to find your field notes when looking to confirm something important a child shared in an interview. An electronic filing system can help ensure that this does not happen to you. Specifically, if you have not already done so, you will want to create a master project folder; you can name this folder the name you assign to your case study. Within that master folder you should have another folder containing the scholarly literature you reviewed and your rationale/research proposal.

Another folder within the master study folder should contain approval for the study, including signed guardian consent forms and child assents. Recall that you must ask children for their assent before they participate in each research activity (i.e., an activity that is different from normal classroom activities is primarily for research purposes). Creating and printing a spreadsheet with each child participant's name on the y axis and each research activity (e.g., drawing interview, walking-tour interview) on the x axis can support you in keeping track of child assent. You can then take a photograph of this spreadsheet and file it in the approval folder.

Similarly, you should create folders for each of the types of data you plan to collect. Mrs. Rousseau has created each of the following folders within her master folder: (1) reflective journal entries, (2) MMRP surveys, (3) drawing interviews, (4) walking-tour interviews, and (5) field notes. Mrs. Rousseau can easily file her journal entries and her colleague's field notes into their respective folders.

Her MMRP surveys folder will include scanned PDFs or photographs of the children's completed MMRPs as well as a master spreadsheet containing their scores. The drawing interviews folder will include photographs of the children's drawings as well as mp4 files from the recorded interviews and, eventually, written transcripts from the mp4 files. The walking-tour interviews folder will similarly include mp4 files from the recorded interviews and, eventually, written transcripts from the mp4 files.

Reaching a Point of Saturation

How do you know when you have collected enough data to reach solid conclusions? In part, your data collection is constrained by the amount of time you have allotted to your study. In Mrs. Rousseau's case, this is four weeks. However, because the conclusions you reach are intended to positively influence your practice, it is crucial that those conclusions are sound. Therefore, there may be instances in which you need to extend your study to collect additional data. At other times, you may reach a point of saturation before the time you allotted for data collection is up.

Saturation occurs when the information you glean from your study becomes largely repetitive; put differently, new information is no longer surfacing in the data you collect (Creswell & Poth, 2018; Merriam & Tisdell, 2016). As you will read in later chapters focusing on data analysis, it is important to read through your data soon after collecting it. This preliminary form of analysis can alert you to new information. If for several days your data fails to reveal any new information, you have likely reached a point of saturation. This may be a good time to stop collecting data.

Say, for example, in Mrs. Rousseau's case, that after three and a half weeks of interviewing and observing her students, multiple sources of data indicate that nearly all children in her study enjoy the reading workshop and phonics portions of her literacy block but would prefer not to participate in the phonemic awareness component. The students offer several reasons for disliking the phonemic awareness instruction as well as suggestions for making it more enjoyable.

Mrs. Rousseau reviews collected data at the end of each day or soon thereafter and discovers that the children are saying the same things over and over. Additionally, journal entries and field notes fail to yield any new insights. It is fairly safe to say that the study has reached a point of saturation; she can move on from collecting data to more closely analyzing and drawing conclusions from it. It is not always possible given time constraints to reach a clear point of saturation; however, doing so is optimal.

SUMMARY

This chapter identifies places in prevalent daily literacy routines where you might be able feasibly to collect data. Once you have identified a strong rationale for conducting your study, developed clear questions to guide it, and identified the data you will collect to answer those questions, you are ready to begin planning for data collection. One teacher's process of making room for data collection—namely, that of Mrs. Rousseau—was explained in detail. You may be able to make modifications to Mrs. Rousseau's process to support your own investigation.

It is important to gather multiple types of data for triangulation. Mrs. Rousseau employed five types of data to support her case study: daily reflective journal entries, pre- and post-motivation surveys, drawing interviews, walking tours, and field notes. She also included multiple people in the data collection process (i.e., students, co-teacher, teaching assistant, guardians). Including several sources of information supports the trustworthiness of your process and makes collection more feasible.

Table 5.1. Activity 5

My Data Collection Plan Exercise
1. Title of Study:  Figure 5.1. *James Dangora* 
2. Rationale (Synthesize why you are conducting the study and your main aims):
3. Research Question(s):
4. Duration of the Study (in weeks):
5. Data Type: Source: When and How Data Will Be Collected:

It is possible to embed most aspects of data collection into your existing daily routines without adding hours to your workday. Intentionally scheduling your time and organizing your data collection procedures can save you time and energy. Chunking your day into three parts (before school, during school, after school) to accomplish tasks is one strategy you might employ to support your process. A systematic approach to collecting and organizing data will assist you in determining when you have reached a point of saturation; regularly reviewing the data you have collected will give you a sense of when you are no longer gaining new insights.

REFERENCES

Creswell, J. W., & Poth, C. N. (2018). *Qualitative inquiry and research design: Choosing among five approaches* (4th ed.). Sage.

Dana, N. F., & Yendol-Hoppey, D. (2020). *The reflective educator's guide to classroom research: Learning to teach and teaching to learn through practitioner inquiry* (4th ed.). Corwin.

Kuh, L. P., & Ponte, I. C. (2017). The power of intention: Reconsidering everyday early childhood practices. *Exchange*, May/June 2017, 8–13.

Marinak, B. A., Malloy, J. B., Gambrell, L. B., & Mazzoni, S. A. (2015). Me and my reading profile: A tool for assessing early reading motivation. *The Reading Teacher*, 69(1), 51–62. DOI: https://doi.org/10.1002/trtr.1362

Merriam, S. B., & Tisdell, E. J. (2016). *Qualitative research: A guide to design and implementation* (4th ed.). Jossey-Bass.

Powell, A. S. (2009). *The cornerstone: Classroom management that makes teaching more effective, efficient, and enjoyable* (2nd ed.). Due Season Press.

Chapter 6

I Have to Analyze All of This Too?!

Drafting an Analysis Plan That Works for You

Beth Fornauf and Joy Dangora Erickson

"Well, I guess I'm OK at reading."—Daniel, age 6

First-grade student Daniel made this comment while engaged in a drawing interview. Daniel quickly moved on from his comment to describe an aspect of his reading intervention that he really enjoyed, so the interviewer did not interrupt the flow of the interview to probe more specifically about what he meant. However, in reviewing the interview transcript that night, the interviewer highlighted the statement and made a note on the next week's interview protocol to ask Daniel more about how he perceived his reading capabilities (e.g., what he did well, what he wanted to improve).

This is a major benefit of *formative data analysis*, a process in which you review data as you collect it in order to consider next steps for your research and instruction (Dana & Yendol-Hoppey, 2020). Reviewing the data you collect each day—even if only very quickly—can support you in making important decisions.

According to motivation theory (e.g., SEVT; see Chapter 1), how Daniel perceives himself as a reader is likely to contribute to his motivation to read and complete related tasks. If he is willing to discuss the intricacies of his views with a trusted interviewer, what the interviewer learns from that discussion may enable his teacher(s) (and potentially others) to better support his developing motivation across reading activities and, in turn, his developing reading proficiency and achievement.

Summative data analysis, on the other hand, occurs at the end of a research project and involves a careful review of your entire corpus of data (Dana & Yendol-Hoppey, 2020). Systematic review of your entire data set not only enhances your findings but also allows you to see the big picture and draw research-based conclusions. This chapter will discuss several benefits of formative and summative data analysis and assist you in developing a plan for analyzing your data set. Formative and summative analysis can play important roles in analyzing quantitative and qualitative data.

ANALYZING QUANTITATIVE DATA

As discussed in Chapter 2, collecting quantitative data can be a useful source of information for your inquiry. In conjunction with qualitative data, quantitative data (e.g., survey results) can help you get a sense of students' overall reading motivation, and/or make comparisons at the beginning and end of your inquiry. This type of data can be analyzed both formatively and summatively to inform not only your instruction but also next steps—even changes and additions—to your inquiry process.

In Chapter 4 you learned about the *Me and My Reading Profile* (MMRP) (Marinak et al., 2015), a valid and reliable means of measuring reading motivation for early elementary students (grades K–2). Analyzing results from the MMRP and/or any other valid and reliable reading motivation survey at the start of your study can provide you with insight into students' overall reading motivation. The results of this formative analysis can help you make decisions about where to focus your inquiry, and help you develop questions you might have about specific students in one or more specific contexts.

For example, if a child indicated on the MMRP that they do not enjoy reading out loud in front of others, the teacher researcher might decide to conduct observations of the child in those situations, paying particular attention to their communication (e.g., verbal, behavioral). Additionally, or alternatively, the interviewer might ask the child about reading aloud in an interview. A stimulated recall procedure (e.g., Lyle, 2003) where the interviewer focuses questions on a specific instance (e.g., a video clip of the child reading out loud from the previous day) could be employed to gain a better sense of the event from the child's perspective.

Data from the MMRP could also be analyzed summatively. A teacher researcher may wish to administer the same survey at the study's conclusion and analyze the results (see Chapter 8 for a step-by-step explanation of how to do this using Microsoft Excel). Knowing how students' general motivation progressed from the beginning to the end of the study can inform future instructional choices and generate new questions.

For example, if students' overall motivation decreased over the course of the study, the teacher can try to determine when and why student engagement decreased and consider making changes to one or more of the classroom reading activities or programs. If overall motivation increased, the teacher might wonder how to incorporate certain elements that appeared to support the students' motivation more regularly into classroom practices.

Remember, survey data, even from a valid and reliable instrument such as the MMRP, does not offer a full picture of what is happening in your study. Recall from Chapter 2 that a primary advantage of the case study method is in drawing from multiple data sources. Data sources should be chosen to work together to help the teacher researcher draw trustworthy conclusions and substantiate results. However, quantitative data, including results from the MMRP, can be used in both formative and summative analysis. Furthermore, in combination with qualitative data, both types of analyses can be informative and yield meaningful results.

ANALYZING QUALITATIVE DATA

As with quantitative data, analyzing qualitative data both during and at the conclusion of an inquiry has many benefits. However, beginning researchers are often overwhelmed at the sheer amount of data qualitative research methods produce. This is where formative data analysis can be particularly useful; not only can it help with organizing data as it is collected, but it also provides a permanent product of the day-to-day experiences of students.

Reviewing data each day can support the thoroughness of your investigation and/or send you in directions you might not have gone otherwise. For example, imagine that you observed a child's enthusiasm for a specific book or series during your literacy block. This might prompt you to generate questions for an interview about the root of the student's enjoyment. You may then be able to use this information to cultivate the child's interest in other subject areas.

Summative analysis allows you to see more clearly the big picture. Though originally you might focus on analyzing data specific to each individual child (assuming there is more than one), your next step might be to look for commonalities and points of divergence across individuals. If, for example, none of the students in your study enjoy a specific aspect of the intervention (e.g., word building), you might question what can be done to make that aspect more motivationally supportive. On the other hand, if all students enjoy something specific, you might question how you can leverage that aspect of instruction in other parts of the program/day.

Additionally, or alternatively, if studying a single child, you might begin by reviewing data generated exclusively from that child. Next you might analyze data about the child from other sources (e.g., teacher, guardian) and look for commonalities and points of divergence. If multiple sources suggest that the child is especially interested in reading books/learning about a certain topic, perhaps more books on that topic can be integrated into the program (i.e., instruction can be made more personal).

Note that with both formative and summative analysis, across both quantitative and qualitative data, you are looking to understand what is happening with your students as they interact with the context, and specific elements of your study (e.g., a specific program, instructional approaches, materials). While you may identify challenges and successes, keep in mind that classroom inquiry is about examining your practice to understand how best to support students; your inquiry may alert you to areas where students are struggling, but your analysis should reveal how you as a teacher are empowered to innovate and adapt to support each child.

CREATING A PLAN FOR ANALYSIS

Recall the story of Mrs. Rousseau's inquiry from Chapter 5, in which she crafted a plan to collect various types of data throughout the school day. Her questions were as follows:

1. What do these children understand to be the advantages and/or disadvantages of participating in their daily literacy block?
2. If permitted to choose, would they participate in it? Why or why not?
3. How might the literacy block be shaping their overall motivation to read?

To answer these questions, Mrs. Rousseau drew data from a variety of sources, including daily reflective journal entries, survey scores from the MMRP (during the first and last weeks of her 4-week inquiry), drawing interviews, walking-tour interviews, and field notes. Although there will be large amounts of data, formative analysis will help Mrs. Rousseau stay organized and informed as she works through her data collection and help her prepare for summative analysis at the end of her inquiry. To help illustrate this process, consider the following plan Mrs. Rousseau might make for analyzing her data over the duration of her inquiry.

Weeks 1 and 2: Initial Insights and Informative Interviews

In addition to working out kinks in the data collection schedule described in Chapter 5, the first week can be spent establishing routines for reviewing data. During the first few days of her inquiry, Mrs. Rousseau can focus her data collection efforts on keeping up with reflective journal entries (during prep blocks or after school) and collecting field notes from her co-teacher. The combination of writing her reflective journals and reviewing field notes can help Mrs. Rousseau gain initial insights into what is happening with students during her literacy block.

For example, in reading through these data, she may notice commonalities or patterns between her observations and those of her co-teacher. Perhaps they both notice the same student avoiding certain tasks. Mrs. Rousseau could highlight or "flag" the tasks the student seems to avoid and ask specifically about those during a drawing interview later in the week.

Or, maybe they each note that many students tend to exhibit more off-task behaviors during the last 20 minutes of the block (e.g., asking to leave the room, chatting with friends). Mrs. Rousseau may want to spend more time observing specifically what students are doing during this time period or try offering a different type of high-engagement activity or task during that time the following week.

In addition to field notes and journals, Mrs. Rousseau will also want to schedule a time for students to take the MMRP during the first week. She can later use summative analysis to examine performance across timepoints (pre- and post-inquiry). However, she does not have to wait until the conclusion of her study to analyze these data. She can keep track of initial scores in a spreadsheet, look at overall patterns in reading motivation across all students, and consider things she may want to attend to in her observations and journal entries, as well as possible questions for interviews with individual students.

Finally, Mrs. Rousseau can review her initial corpus of data to refine questions for her student interviews. Information that she has gleaned from her observations and those of her co-teacher can also help her prioritize which students to interview first and indicate the responses that the interviewer should focus on eliciting to inform her instruction and address her research questions (i.e., perceived benefits and costs related to the literacy block).

In the second week of the inquiry, Mrs. Rousseau can continue with routines established during the first week, but also, through further analysis, refine the data she needs to collect in future weeks. In particular, she will want to listen to and transcribe (or hire an outside service to transcribe) the drawing interviews, and look through student drawings, making initial "jottings," or notes, during the process (Emerson et al., 2011). These quick notes can serve to flag important information on which Mrs. Rousseau may want to follow up and/or help identify initial patterns in student responses that she may want to revisit during the summative analysis phase.

In addition to noting patterns and important information, reviewing the interviews and drawings can also help Mrs. Rousseau identify any missing information that the interview protocol is not addressing. For example, if students willingly talk at length about their favorite parts of the reading block but are reluctant to discuss activities they find less engaging, Mrs. Rousseau can either amend the interview questions and/or follow up with individual students to get this information.

Week 3: Digging Deeper and Making Connections

During the third week Mrs. Rousseau will begin to conduct walking-tour interviews. As discussed in Chapter 4, these interviews work well in conjunction with drawing interviews to help provide a more nuanced understanding of a child's likes and dislikes related to a particular program or activity. Thus, teacher researchers need to be sure they have done their "homework" in preparation for conducting this type of interview. Reviewing transcripts, drawings, and jottings from previous interviews will be helpful in refining the walking-tour protocol and making sure each student is comfortable sharing their perceptions and feelings.

In the week or two between the interviews, Mrs. Rousseau may want to target some of her observations and journals to focus on particular students. Depending on the data collected during drawing interviews, she may want to be sure to observe certain students during particular sections of the literacy block, or to attend to tasks and activities that students do or do not engage in.

In addition to attending to students who may be struggling, she can review her roster to make sure she is collecting adequate data on all students. Because her research questions address all of her students, she should take care to include ample documentation on each one of them, and coordinate with her co-teacher to ensure collection of these data.

Finally, Mrs. Rousseau can begin to watch and transcribe the walking-tour interviews. As with the drawing interviews, it may be helpful to take jottings during this process in preparation for upcoming summative analysis. At this point, one might begin to notice more obvious patterns in the data sources from a particular student. These can be noted in jottings and be analyzed in more detail using coding methods (e.g., Saldaña, 2016) during summative analysis.

Week 4: Putting It All Together

During the final week of your inquiry, you will begin to wrap up your data collection and begin summative analysis of your data. In Mrs. Rousseau's case, she will want to administer the MMRP a final time during week four so that she can compare students' motivation pre- and post-inquiry. A detailed plan for analyzing MMRP results using a basic statistical analysis technique is offered in Chapter 8.

In addition to administering the MMRP, Mrs. Rousseau will continue with reflective journals and comparing her observations any field notes of her co-teacher(s). These observations can still inform her final walking-tour interviews, which should also be completed this week. She will need to transcribe these interviews (or hire an outside source to do so) in order to make sure that her entire qualitative data set is ready for summative analysis. She should also continue to look for patterns across sources.

For example, if Mrs. Rousseau has noticed an improvement in a student's overall interest in completing word work over the course of the study, she may want to ask specifically about this during the walking-tour interview. Because of the nature of walking-tour interviews, Mrs. Rousseau will have the opportunity to understand the "why" behind the students' observed increase in motivation for specific tasks.

Once all qualitative data have been collected, Mrs. Rousseau can begin her summative analysis. She will need to gather and organize all data—journal entries, field notes (complete with highlights and jottings), transcripts, and any videos—so that she can review the entire corpus. While this may seem overwhelming at first, this process will help her recall details she might have forgotten and/or notice new ones. At this stage, she is not yet drawing conclusions; rather, she is simply taking note of what appears to have happened with her students and her instruction over the course of her inquiry (Dana & Yendol-Hoppey, 2020).

In the next chapter, you will learn much more about summative qualitative data analysis. A specific approach for analyzing data, identifying patterns across sources, and interpreting results will be outlined.

SUMMARY

This chapter introduced the concepts of formative and summative data analysis. Formative and summative analyses can be used to make sense of both quantitative and qualitative data. Ongoing (formative) data analysis better positions teacher researchers to make changes to a study as it is unfolding. Multiple examples of how formative analysis might inform an in-process study were offered in this chapter. For example, reviewing quantitative survey data at the start of a study can support the teacher researcher in deciding who and what to pay close attention to during interviews and/or observations.

The more thorough analysis that takes place at the end of the case study (summative analysis) supports the teacher researcher in systematically combing through the data set in its entirety as a means of making sure nothing of importance is missed or misinterpreted. Both types of analysis play an important role in drawing sound conclusions and making reasonable inferences. Using Mrs. Rousseau's data collection plan from Chapter 5, this chapter also identified and discussed when and how formative and summative analysis techniques might best be employed in Mrs. Rousseau's study.

Table 6.1. Activity 6

Data Analysis Plan Exercise

Use this table to create a plan for data analysis. Begin by adding enough rows to represent each week of your inquiry. Next, for each week add a row for each data source and one or two more for summative analysis. Complete each column to the right of "Week" amended as needed as you progress through your study. The fourth column will help ensure that you are including both formative and summative types of analysis in your study. You may be better positioned to add your summative (final) steps after reading Chapters 7 and 8. The final two columns are optional, but may be useful if you wish to track your analysis, as well as make notes or changes about your inquiry. Several example entries are listed under "Week 1" for your reference.

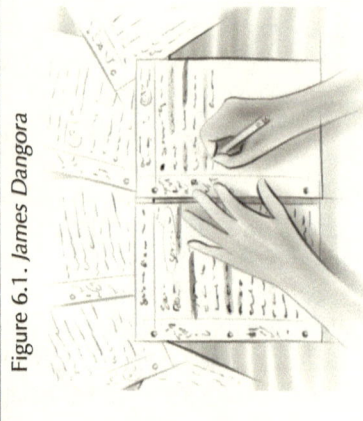

Figure 6.1. *James Dangora*

Week	Data Collected	How Will I Analyze This Data?	Formative or Summative?	Complete?	Notes
1	Field Notes	Read through; highlight areas of interest; make notes to track thinking	Formative	Y	
	Reflective Journals	Read through; highlight areas of interest; compare to field notes; make notes to track thinking	Formative	Y	

MMRP	Review all scores; look for patterns across students; compare to field notes and reflective journals; make notes to track thinking	Formative	Y	Three students reported disliking reading out loud; closely observe these students when reading out loud during small group instruction; ask them about reading out loud during interviews
Drawing Interview	Listen to and transcribe; look over drawings; note anything of interest; compare to field notes, reflective journals, and MMRP; make notes to track thinking	Formative	N	Two of the three students shared that they did not enjoy reading out loud during small group instruction.

REFERENCES

Dana, N. F., & Yendol-Hoppey, D. (2020). *The reflective educator's guide to classroom research: Learning to teach and teaching to learn through practitioner inquiry* (4th ed.). Corwin Press.

Emerson, R. M., Fretz, R. I., & Shaw, L. L. (2011). *Writing ethnographic fieldnotes*. University of Chicago Press.

Lyle, J. (2003). Stimulated recall: A report on its use in naturalistic research. *British Educational Research Journal, 29*(6), 861–878. https://doi.org/10.1080/0141192032000137349

Marinak, B. A., Malloy, J. B., Gambrell, L. B., & Mazzoni, S. A. (2015). Me and My Reading Profile: A tool for assessing early reading motivation. *The Reading Teacher, 69*(1), 51–62. https:/doi.org/10.1002/trtr.1362

Saldaña, J. (2016). *The coding manual for qualitative researchers (*3rd ed.). Sage.

Chapter 7

Help! I'm Drowning in Data!
Making Sense of Qualitative Data

Joy Dangora Erickson and Alessandra E. Ward

"Take a picture! Take a picture so we don't forget!"—Gemma, age 6

After learning that the research team (i.e., teacher, professor, student teacher) often took pictures of the reading space and what happened in it, Gemma reminded the team to regularly photograph aspects of her reading time that she deemed important to remember. On this particular day, she had just finished writing and drawing in her journal about a decodable text she had recently completed. She wanted everyone to be able to look back at her work product.

Gemma's language is notable. "So we don't forget!" suggests she saw herself as a contributing member of the research project. Her frequent reminders and the reminders of other children to document that which occurred over the course of the study served the project well in that the visuals produced assisted the team in better describing the instructional methods, tools, work products, and children's behaviors noted in other forms of data (e.g., field notes, journal entries, interviews). The photographs also came in handy when it came time to report findings; the team integrated some of the photos into their final case report and slide presentations.

Gemma's teacher and the researcher working with her pasted their photos at the bottom of reflective journal entries and added brief descriptions (see example in Figure 7.1). Every few days or so, they would review the reflective journal entries as well as other freshly collected pieces of data and jot down important ideas that came to mind. Recall that this process of

Reflective Diary/Journal Entry

Joy D. Erickson
5/5/2021
Gemma and Lil's ERI Session (9:00am-9:30am)

During this virtual observation I noticed that both Gemma and Lil more actively participated in particular aspects of their reading intervention. Overall, Lil was quicker to comply with her interventionist's requests. Specifically, she got materials out immediately when asked and almost always raised her hand to answer questions. Gemma also complied with most requests, but it took her a bit more time and she occasionally needed directions repeated.

Gemma appeared to enter the room more enthusiastically than Lil. She immediately began telling the interventionist about her weekend. Lil remarked to Gemma that she wished their other friend, Linn, who remained in the classroom was with them. Lil looked a bit down as she took her seat.

When I interview Lil next week, I will ask her more about this. Specifically, I am wondering if Lil regularly misses Linn during ERI lessons and, if she does, might that sense of loss be influencing her motivation for the program? Alternatively, might occasionally inviting Linn to join Lil better support Lil's motivation for the program? Though I will not directly ask these questions as not to influence Lil's answer, I will look to see if Lil mentions Linn in our interview on her own. If she does not, I might ask her who Linn is and why she told Gemma that she wished Linn could come with them to intervention.

Both girls perked up for the letter, keyword, sound drill. They seemed to like how the interventionist sped up the drill as they went on. Though Gemma struggled more than Lil (which is typical), she appeared to maintain her level of enthusiasm for the drill, smiling often. Gemma also persisted until the end.

When the interventionist asked the girls to get out their ERI books, they both did so in a timely manner. Lil had her book out and ready first. The interventionist announced that each member of the group (5 children) would read a page aloud. Lil sighed at this request; it appeared as though she was not excited to participate in this task. Both girls became distracted while the other students in the group were reading and needed to be reminded when it was their turn. When I interview Lil next week, I will ask her specifically how she feels about the round robin approach to reading used today. I am wondering if her sigh was a signal of her feelings about this aspect of the intervention.

Photograph(s) Taken Today:

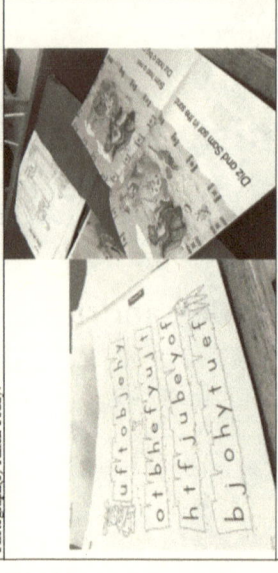

(ERI Book)

(Sound-Mapping Practice)

Figure 7.1. Journal Entries with Descriptions

reviewing data as it is being collected is called formative data analysis (Dana & Yendol-Hoppey, 2020).

The two women jotted down their ideas using the comment feature in their word processing program. The comment feature can be convenient; however, some researchers prefer to audio record their thinking and save the mp4 files in a folder. When it comes to formative data analysis, you should do what works best for you. However you decide to go about it, regular systematic review of your data can keep you from getting lost in it.

FORMATIVE DATA ANALYSIS

The *formative data analysis* (Dana & Yendol-Hoppey, 2020) techniques just described supported Gemma's teacher and her research team in making some important decisions about their project as it unfolded. Specifically, the team's many jottings generated in response to their continuous review of collected data informed the following aspects of the research process:

- *The questions posed to children during interviews:* ongoing review of data supported the team in determining which ideas they needed more clarification on from individual students (e.g., why a specific student enjoyed/disliked a specific activity). They were able to ask personalized questions because of their ongoing analyses.
- *The number of child interviews conducted:* review of interview transcripts supported the team in determining when an additional follow-up interview was warranted. Several students required a third interview to gain a more thorough understanding of their perceptions of the reading program.
- *The number of observations completed*: review of field notes and reflective journal entries sometimes revealed that one or more participants were receiving more attention than others. Additional observations of several students were required to better describe their experiences and behaviors.
- *The types of data collected*: on one occasion jottings spurred the research team to create and collect a questionnaire for guardians. This questionnaire was not originally part of the research plan but added another valuable perspective.

Additionally, the research team's formative analysis supported their final, or summative data analysis. Specifically, the team's jottings facilitated deep thinking and kept ideas fresh in their minds; they informed the themes that were finalized later in the analysis process. For example, multiple jottings pertained to the potential impact of round-robin reading on the children's motivation to participate in the program. These jottings in conjunction with later stages of data analysis (e.g., coding, memoing) led to the development of a major theme discussed in the final case report—namely, that of "round-robin reading as demotivator."

SUMMATIVE DATA ANALYSIS

While formative data analysis typically occurs throughout your study, *summative data analysis* is the systematic process you complete at the end of your study to make sure you have not missed anything important and to make connections among findings. Specifically, your process of summative data analysis will consist largely of (1) *coding* your data, or breaking it up into small meaningful chunks, and (2) *memoing* on your work, or identifying and discussing in writing your analysis process as well as any patterns you notice upon chunking your data (Creswell & Poth, 2018; Dana & Yendol-Hoppey, 2020; Strauss & Corbin, 1998).

In the pages that follow, a modified version of Dana and Yendol-Hoppey's (2020) method for summatively analyzing qualitative data is discussed in relation to the case study referenced at the start of this chapter involving Gemma. The study explored three young English Learners' (EL) (i.e., two kindergarten students [Gemma and Lil]; one first-grade student [Rocky]) motivation for their pull-out reading intervention program. The research team identified the following questions to guide their study:

1. What do these children understand to be the advantages and/or disadvantages of participating in their reading intervention program?
2. If permitted to choose, would they participate in it? Why or why not?
3. What do children's behaviors during the intervention suggest about their motivation for the program?

Over the course of a semester (12 weeks) the team conducted five close observations of each child's engagement in the intervention (i.e., field notes), completed 36 reflective journal entries, and interviewed each child twice with two different participatory approaches (i.e., drawing interview, walking-tour interview). The interviews were transcribed by an outside service. The data collected was largely composed of words to be analyzed. However, photos taken during the inquiry were referenced as needed to jog the researchers' memories.

Description

The first stage in summative qualitative data analysis is description (Dana & Yendol-Hoppey, 2020). This is where you and anyone working with you read over the entire data set (including your formative analysis jottings). It is good practice to review the summary of relevant scholarly literature you generated at the start of your inquiry before poring over your own data; this can spark some initial insights. Your main objective during this stage is to hold your research question(s) in your mind and describe anything in the data set that jumps out at you in relation to them. It can be helpful to complete this step with another person.

Upon reviewing their research questions, their synthesis of the scholarly literature, and their complete data set, the research team briefly listed and discussed the following main points:

- All children reported that reading was an important skill to acquire.
- Two of the three children reported that they valued learning to read in the intervention.
- One child indicated that she would not attend the intervention if given the choice; she was the most competent reader of the three.
- All children reported enjoying some intervention activities and not enjoying other activities.
- All three children reported that there were some books provided in the intervention that they enjoyed reading and others they did not.

Generating this descriptive list of noticings offered an overview of the data in relation to their research questions and prepared the team for the more detailed analysis to come.

Sense Making

Sense making is the second stage in Dana and Yendol-Hoppey's (2020) method of summative qualitative data analysis. It is within this stage that you zoom in on your data by chunking small relevant bits of information and then make decisions about whether and how the chunks fit together. For the EL case study of motivation, the research team decided to first examine their data in relation to each of the three child-participants.

To do this, they wrote each research question on a white index card and then each child's name on another white index card. Next, they arranged the six cards in a 3X3 table on the floor (research questions along the top and children's names down the left-hand side). This visual representation supported them in centering what they were looking for in the data (see Figure 7.2).

Each member of the three-person research team (i.e., teacher, professor, student teacher) was assigned a child-participant. They printed their own hard copies of all data (i.e., field notes, reflective journal entries, interview transcripts) and searched for their assigned child's perceived advantages and disadvantages of intervention participation. Using a green highlighter for advantages and a pink one for disadvantages, the researchers read through the data and highlighted chunks relevant to the first research question.

Afterward, they searched through the data for their assigned child's report of whether they would attend the intervention or not if given the choice. The child's answer (i.e., yes or no) was highlighted in yellow. Third, they read through all data for evidence of engaged and disengaged behaviors; engaged behaviors (e.g., enthusiasm, question posing, maintained focus) were highlighted in purple and disengaged behaviors (e.g., expressed disinterest, apathy, lack of focus) were highlighted in orange.

Once this initial step of breaking up the data into relevant chunks was complete, the team gave short names, or *codes*, to the chunks (Creswell & Poth, 2018). Codes can consist of participants' own words and/or be words or phrases generated by the researcher. For example, a main disadvantage of intervention involvement reported by Lil was not being able to read with her close friend; after highlighting Lil's words, "I want to stay and read with

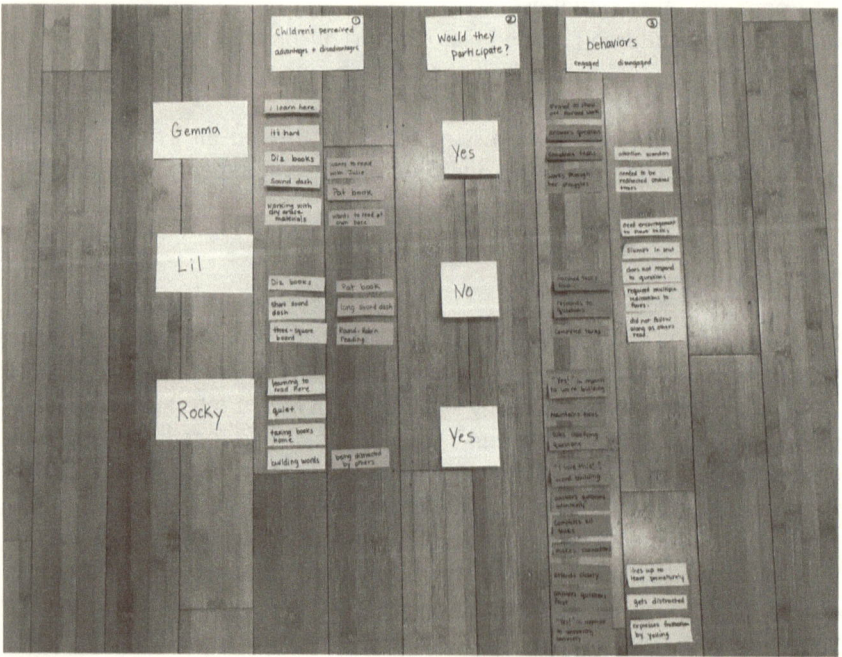

Figure 7.2. Early Coding Table

Linn" in pink, the researcher initially coded this excerpt, "wants to read with Linn." All codes generated by the team were then written on color-coded sticky notes and added to the 3X3 table (see Figure 7.2).

At this point the team looked for overlap in their sticky notes; were there places where multiple sticky notes could be represented by a single code? The team found that oftentimes there were. For example, the initial codes "'I love this!'," "'Yes!'," and "excited to show off finished work" were replaced with the single code, "enthusiasm for intervention." The condensed set of

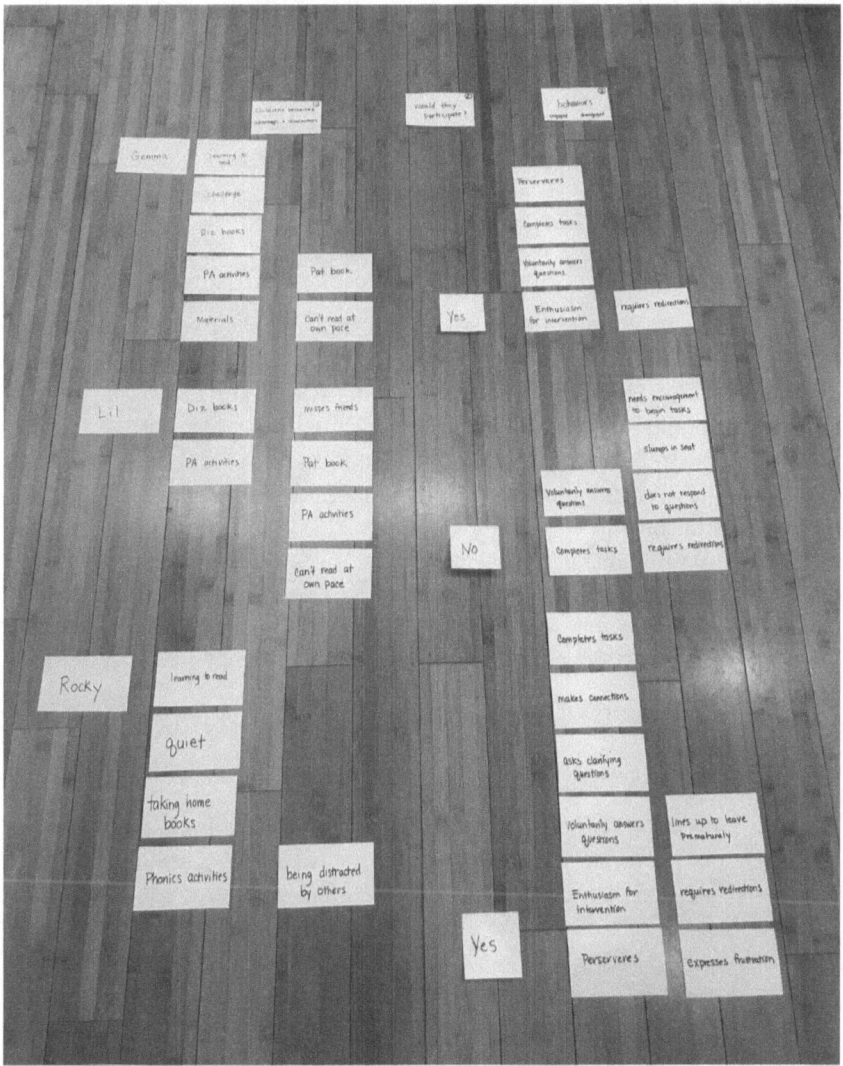

Figure 7.3. Revised Coding Table

codes was written on a sheet of paper, and the group recoded their data using the condensed code list. They then made a final index card for each recoded chunk and arranged them in the table (see Figure 7.3).

To document the process they had used to refine their codes, the group generated a *memo* together. Researchers memo at various times throughout the analysis process to explain their process and/or what they see unfolding in the data. This process-oriented memo (Strauss & Corbin, 1998) explained how and why the team created the table on the floor and how they decided upon their final set of codes. In another theoretical memo, they discussed some exciting patterns that emerged in the visual data. These included:

- Rocky and Gemma, two students who reported enjoying the intervention, reported twice as many perceived benefits of participating than Lil who indicated that she did not want to participate.
- Lil displayed more disengaged behaviors and less engaged behaviors than both Rocky and Gemma.
- Rocky displayed the widest range of engaged behaviors.

The team noticed that observations of students' intervention behaviors often aligned with their self-reports about their motivation for the reading intervention. Put differently, the two students who reported wanting to participate in the intervention showed more engaged behaviors during observations of them in the intervention than the student who reported not wanting to attend. This triangulation of findings supported the team in drawing trustworthy conclusions.

Working with a team, representing data visually, and memoing as you complete steps in the analysis process can all help you reach sound conclusions. However, the team decided to take one additional step to ensure they were arriving at sound conclusions—namely, they engaged in a form of peer review.

Peer Review

Peer review can further boost the trustworthiness of your findings and conclusions. It is not a discrete step in Dana and Yendol-Hoppey's (2020) method of summative data analysis; however, it fits in quite well after you have established a final set of codes. If you are working with a research team, you are well positioned to check your work in this way. If you are working alone, you might ask a peer or colleague to review your work and discuss it with you.

The research team conducting the EL case study engaged in a form of peer review shortly after drafting their process and theoretical memos. Before they got too far into their interpretation of the data, they decided to check to make sure they had accurately coded each child's data with their agreed-upon codes (agreeing upon your final list of codes with another person is also a form of peer review). To do this, they swapped assigned children and obtained fresh copies of the data. Next, they each applied the agreed-upon codes to a new (to them) child. Afterward, they compared their application of codes to those applied by the first researcher.

Though more often than not the two researchers applied the same codes to the data, there were times when they disagreed. For example, in one instance the second reader did not feel a code should be applied to an observation of Lil slumping in her seat; the first reader thought it should. To settle their dispute, they reviewed a photo taken on the same day as the field notes they were coding. The photo captured Lil slumping in her seat during intervention. She appeared disengaged to both readers, so the group decided to keep the code.

In all instances of disagreement the research team decided what to do together. Having someone else code the data and rectifying discrepancies together can substantially increase the trustworthiness of your findings (Creswell & Poth, 2018; Miles et al., 2014). It is important to integrate peer review into your analysis process, and it makes good sense to have someone check your work after you have finished applying a set of codes for the first time.

Interpretation and Implications

Once the EL research team was satisfied with their final coding and the visual representations of the data, they completed the process of interpreting it (Dana & Yendol-Hoppey, 2020). First, they memoed about each child; each member of the research team drafted a memo in which they used their previous memos, visual representations, and raw data to answer the research questions specific to their focus child. Answers to each research question were detailed, observed patterns in the data were described, and multiple relevant pieces of evidence were included (e.g., quote from child, observed behavior) to support claims.

Afterward, they came back together as a team to look for patterns across memos/children. They looked for points of convergence in the data (e.g., all students enjoyed reading a particular book series, all students did not enjoy round-robin reading) and points of divergence (e.g., leaving her classroom was a serious demotivator for Lil but not the other two students). They discussed together what these points of convergence and divergence might mean for each child, for the group, and for the program. The teacher member of the research team took notes during this meeting and organized the whole-group findings into a fourth memo.

Finally, the team was ready to draw implications from their findings (Dana & Yendol-Hoppey, 2020). They began by generating a list informed by their findings of what might be largely true about young ELs specific to school reading programs. Their list included the following points:

- Many children can report out on what they appreciate and do not appreciate about school reading programs when the methods used to probe their views make sense to them.
- Children are motivated and demotivated by different things; when it comes to supporting motivation, one-size-fits-all reading programs are unlikely to fit anyone perfectly.
- Children's behaviors during reading lessons often match the degree to which they are motivated to participate in the program.

Next, the teacher member of the research team discussed with the group and listed what she had learned about her own practice. Among her list of points were the following high-priority actions:

- I should be regularly monitoring students' (1) general motivation to read and (2) motivation for their reading intervention(s) to better support their developing motivation and reading proficiency.
- There are several relatively simple changes to my practice that I can try immediately (e.g., permit Lil to read with a friend from time to time, incorporate more series books) to better support students' motivation.
- I need to figure out a way to monitor my students' reading without requiring them to read round-robin style.

Finally, the research team pondered what they had learned about schooling in general. The following points were on their list:

- Children often have minimal say about the programs they are enrolled in and that which occurs within them. They should have more say in all matters that impact them.
- The traditional structure of schooling does not encourage feedback from children; this appears especially true for certain populations (e.g., young children, ELs). Program-specific feedback from children should be invited and appreciated.
- Schools, mirroring the larger U.S. society, appear to value supporting children's reading skill acquisition more than supporting their motivation to read and learn. Both should be highly valued.

The teacher member of the research team organized all implications into a final implications memo. At the end of this summative analysis process the research team had generated one process memo, four findings memos (one per child and one describing all three children), and one implications memo in total. The five memos would serve them well in their efforts to share what they had learned from the study with others.

SUMMARY

This chapter outlines suggested steps for making sense of qualitative data, including formative data analysis (analysis that is ongoing throughout data collection) and summative data analysis (which occurs after collection is complete). Formative analysis may include reviewing data collected that day or week and jotting down preliminary ideas.

Dana and Yendol-Hoppey's method of summative analysis is referenced; a peer review step was added to the method to support teacher researchers in arriving at trustworthy conclusions and implications. The first step, description, involves teacher researchers reviewing the entire data set and articulating its main points. In the second step, sense making, they take the data apart and then chunk it back together by assigning initial codes and refining those

Table 7.1. Activity 7

Sense Making Practice Exercise	
Complete the stages of summative analysis with an excerpt from an observation in the EL study. • First, use the prompts below to analyze the data specific to Gemma only. • Next, repeat the process analyzing the data specific to Lil.	Figure 7.4. *James Dangora* 

Focus on the following research question:
What do children's behaviors during the intervention suggest about their motivation for the program?

1. **DESCRIPTION:** Read over the excerpt and make a list of anything that jumps out at you in the column next to it.

The interventionist asks the kids to get out the book *Bud the Pup*. Lil and Gemma do this quickly.

The interventionist asks the group to identify and explain various parts of the book (e.g., cover, title page). Both girls raise their hands to respond to questions. They respond eagerly and accurately when called. They appear engaged.

The interventionist asks each member of the group (five students total) to each take turns reading aloud a page from the book.

Engagement appears to break down as the girls wait for their turn to read. Lil slumps in her seat and does not follow along as another group member reads. She seems to be frowning at the wall. The interventionist attempts to direct her back to the text: "Lil, your finger needs to be on the page following along."

Lil complies initially, but her eyes begin to wander around the room again as she waits for her turn. Again, the interventionist redirects her: "Lil, we're turning the page now."

Both girls are asked to sit up and "touch" the words as they are read by others. Both girls struggle to follow along. Gemma also looks around the room as other group members slowly work through the text.

Lil gets the chance to read her page and does so fluently: "Diz said, 'Run, Bud!'" She reads accurately and with expression.

It's Gemma's turn next. She struggles to read what's on the page. The interventionist coaches her through the sentence. Lil slouches in her seat again and looks at a poster on the wall to her right.

Gemma also begins to look away from the text as other group members read a page for the second time.

2. **SENSE MAKING:**
   - Grab two highlighters.
   - Highlight Gemma's engaged behaviors as you interpret them in one color and her disengaged behaviors in another color.
   - Code (assign a short description) to each of the highlighted behaviors and write these on sticky notes or note cards.
   - Sort the sticky notes/note cards into two columns on the floor under the headings "engaged" and "disengaged."
   - Decide if the data fits your codes well. Should you omit, combine, or create additional codes?
   - Write a brief memo explaining what you have done, why you have done it, and what you are noticing about the data.

3. **PEER REVIEW:**
   - Ask a friend to code the excerpt.
   - Compare their coding to your own and resolve any discrepancies together.

4. **INTERPRETATION AND IMPLICATIONS:**
   - Based on the excerpt, what might be true about these young ELs (and potentially others) specific to school reading programs?
   - What might the interventionist learn about her practice from this excerpt?
   - What might be true about schooling in general?

codes. Throughout the process, they generate memos to document their specific analysis process and their ideas about what is meaningful.

In the third step, peer review, the team members work together to check one another's ideas, coding, and assumptions as well as resolve disagreements. Next, teacher researchers interpret the data by looking for points of convergence and divergence and thinking about what they mean. Finally, they draw implications from their findings both for practice and for schooling in general.

REFERENCES

Creswell, J. W., & Poth, C. N. (2018). *Qualitative inquiry and research design: Choosing among five approaches* (4th ed.). Sage.

Dana, N. F., & Yendol-Hoppey, D. (2020). *The reflective educator's guide to classroom research: Learning to teach and teaching to learn through practitioner inquiry* (4th ed.). Corwin.

Miles, M. B., Huberman, A. M., & Saldaña, J. (2014). *Qualitative data analysis: A sourcebook of new methods* (3rd ed.). Sage.

Strauss, A., & Corbin, J. (1998). *Basics of qualitative research: Techniques and procedures for developing grounded theory* (2nd ed.). Sage.

Chapter 8

What About Pre- and Post-Motivation Survey Scores? How Might They Support My Conclusions?

Simple Quantitative Data Analysis

Carla M. Evans

"How many points did I get on mine? . . . Is that better?"—Rocky, age 7

Rocky posed this question to his teacher after completing his *Me and My Reading Profile* (MMRP; Marinak et al., 2015) survey for a second time. Rocky's teacher was using the survey to better understand how the general reading motivation of her students changed from fall to winter. Survey results would give her a sense of who might need some extra support finding personally meaningful books and/or recognizing the value in being able to read well.

Rocky and several of his peers participated in a targeted reading intervention in the fall; they were slated to continue the intervention in the spring. If Rocky's and/or his peers' MMRP scores decreased, his teacher and the reading specialist planned to conduct a case study of the students' more specific motivation for the reading intervention program. Rocky's teacher was wise to monitor regularly her students' general motivation to read; she understood clearly that high motivation for reading and related activities supports students' developing proficiency and achievement.

Using the MMRP periodically throughout the year as a temperature check, may help you decide when a more in-depth study is warranted. However, it can also support a study that you have already decided to conduct. For example, if you are curious about how students' general reading motivation is progressing in relation to a program, you might administer the MMRP at the start and end of your study. Though you will not be able to claim definitively that the intervention increased or decreased MMRP scores, if they remain the same or go up, you might reasonably infer that the intervention did not harm students' general motivation to read.

In the sections that follow, you will learn how to complete simple statistical analyses with pre- and post-MMRP scores that can support your case study of motivation. Specifically, this chapter offers step-by-step instructions explaining how to use Excel to generate basic descriptive statistics at the student and class levels (i.e., total score, difference between pre- and post-survey scores, mean, median, and standard deviation). These statistics can assist you in describing if and to what degree your students' general motivation to read differs over the period of time you are studying them.

BRIEF NOTES ABOUT THE MMRP SCORING DESIGN

Before learning how to set up and input data for the MMRP in Excel, it is important to understand the way the MMRP is designed and how it is intended to be scored. This will help ensure you analyze and interpret the data accurately. Here are some high-level observations to inform scoring MMRP responses:

- The MMRP consists of 20 items with a minimum response value of 1 point and a maximum response value of 3 points. Therefore, the lowest score a student can receive on the MMRP is 20 points and the highest score is 60 points.
- Each item corresponds to one of three subscales: 5 items for a child's self-concept as a reader (SC; 15 points possible); 10 items for a child's appreciation of the value of reading (V; 30 points possible); and 5 items for literacy out loud (LO; 15 points possible). Half of the overall points on the MMRP derive from the value of reading subscale. See Marinak et al.'s (2015) article for more information on the development and validation of each subscale.
- The items are administered in random order such that the subscales are not administered all in one clustered set. The scoring guidelines show which items to add together for each subscale.
- The items are variably scaled. This means that for some items the first response is worth 3 points and the third response is worth 1 point, but that is reversed for other items.

- The MMRP scoring guidelines found in Marinak et al.'s (2015) article show which items go with which subscale and how many points go with each response.
- Scoring is based on the total number of points scored by the student on each subscale and overall.

SETTING UP AND INPUTTING DATA INTO EXCEL

After administering the pre- and post-MMRP with a group of students, you will then use Excel to input the three subscale results (self-concept, value, and literacy out loud) and calculate a few descriptive statistics. Figure 8.1 illustrates how to set up an Excel spreadsheet to input the MMRP subscale results for each student on their pre and post survey. The figure also shows the formulas you should use to calculate the total score, difference between pre- and post-MMRP scores, as well as the mean, median, and standard deviation of the difference scores.

Alternatively, you can download a pre-formatted Excel template with pre-populated formulas as shown in this chapter by going to https://docs.google.com/spreadsheets/d/1C5T04JdC-kGdP0qWk4z__1047ip-o7mM/edit?usp=sharing&ouid=117007983446602327158&rtpof=true&sd=true. The first tab includes instructions for inputting data and use of the template.

You'll notice that Figure 8.1 is designed so that each student is listed across the top row. There are seven students in the figure—Students A–G—and they will be referenced as a running example throughout the rest of this chapter to illustrate certain points. You should also notice that each student's Total MMRP Overall Score is calculated as the sum of the three subscale scores. Student A, for example, scored 49 points on the pre-survey and then 54 points on the post survey—both out of 60 possible points. Total points were calculated rather than other metrics that could be used based upon Marinak et al.'s (2015) scoring guide.

The difference between each student's pre- and post-MMRP scores for each subscale and on the Total MMRP Overall Score is then calculated by subtracting the post-score from the pre-score. In the next section, you will learn why you will focus on the difference in points between the pre- and post-survey for the Total MMRP Overall Score and then how to use the subscales as additional information for follow-up.

To calculate the mean, median, and standard deviation of the difference between pre- and post-TOTAL MMRP Overall Score for the class or group of students examined, you will use the Excel formulas as shown in Figure 8.1. You will notice that the data range shown in the figure is cells D12 to P12. This data range will vary depending upon how many students are in your

	A	B	C	D	E	F	G	H	I	J	K	L	M	N	O	P
1			Student A		Student B		Student C		Student D		Student E		Student F		Student G	
2	Subscale/Scale	Total Pts. Possible	Pre	Post	Pre	Post	Pre	Post	Pre	Post	Pre	Post	Pre	Post	Pre	Post
3	Total Self Concept (SC) Subscale (5 items)	15	13	14	12	11	15	15	12	12	5	7	13	13	15	15
4	Total Value (V) Subscale (10 items)	30	23	26	24	25	24	26	21	22	10	12	22	23	30	30
5	Total Literacy Outloud (LO) Subscale (5 items)	15	13	14	11	11	12	13	8	9	5	7	11	5	15	15
6	Total MMRP (OVERALL)	60	49	54	47	47	51	54	41	43	20	26	46	41	60	60
7				=SUM(C3:C5)												
8	Pts. Different Pre/Post SC Subscale		=D3-C3	1		-1		0		0		2		0		0
9	Pts. Different Pre/Post V Subscale		=D4-C4	3		1		2		1		2		1		0
10	Pts. Different Pre/Post LO Subscale		=D5-C5	1		0		1		1		2		-6		0
11	Pts. Different Pre/Post Total MMRP (Overall)		=D6-C6	5		0		3		3		6		-5		0
12	Mean (or Average) of the Pts. Different Pre/Post for Total MMRP (Overall)			1.7	=AVERAGE(D12:P12)											
13	Median of the Pts. Different Pre/Post for Total MMRP (Overall)			3.0	=MEDIAN(D12:P12)											
14	Standard Deviation of the Pts. Different Pre/Post for Total MMRP (Overall)			3.7	=STDEV.S(D12:P12)											

Figure 8.1. Excel Spreadsheet for MMRP

targeted group. The next section will walk you through how to analyze and interpret the descriptive statistics calculated in the Excel spreadsheet.

ANALYZING AND INTERPRETING DATA

Student-Level Analysis and Interpretation

There are two levels of analysis possible from the Excel calculations: student level and class/group level. The student level is critical to understanding each student's individual progress in reading motivation from pre- to post-survey and contains two parts: total score and difference score.

The *total score* is the sum of the three subscales. Recall that students can earn 1, 2, or 3 points on each of the 20 items on the MMRP. The lowest possible score is 20 (all 1's) and the highest possible score is 60 (all 3's). A student with a mixture of 1's and 2's will score in the range of 20–40; a mixture of 2's and 3's will score in the range of 40–60. A score less than 40 may signal a student on the lower range of reading motivation who may need more intensive supports and interventions (e.g., Figure 8.1, Student E). Students toward the upper bound of the score range (i.e., close to 60 points) may not need their motivation monitored as closely.

The *difference score* shows the extent to which each student is making progress or showing growth in reading motivation relative to themselves—not to others. Sometimes it may help to first see these differences depicted graphically. Figure 8.2 is an example bar graph that illustrates difference scores for Students A–G.

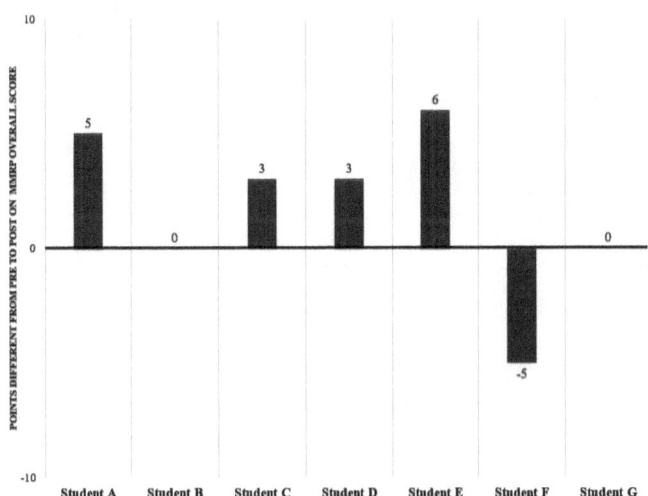

Figure 8.2. Graphic Representation of Differences

If you download the pre-populated Excel template references earlier, a bar graph will automatically populate with results in one of the tabs. This type of quick visual display may help you to identify students you immediately want to examine in more detail. For example, it would make sense to start with Students B, F, and G because Students B and G showed no growth and Student F had a negative result.

A zero difference score means either a student made no growth from pre- to post-survey because there was no growth possible (they scored 60/60 on both pre- and post-survey; Student G in our example) or that a student's reading motivation is unchanged from pre-survey to post-survey (Student B in our example). The expectation is for at least some growth (if possible), as indicated by a difference score of 1 positive point or higher. Larger positive difference scores indicate more progress or growth.

One thing to note, however, when analyzing and interpreting difference scores is that students who score lower initially out of 60 points have the potential to have larger positive growth before they hit the ceiling of the survey (see Student E). That said, larger relative growth to other students in the class or group is not limited to initially lower scoring students (see Student A). Other students may have more modest, yet positive growth relative to others in their class/group as indicated by positive differences between pre and post (see Students C and D).

Not all students will show growth from pre- to post-survey. Student F in our example shows a student who scored 46 on the pre-survey and 39 on the post-survey with a -5 difference between the scores. Examining the subscale score differences between pre and post, it becomes clear that the reason for the negative score relates to the Literacy Out Loud subscale alone. This subscale focuses on interactions about literacy such as listening, speaking, and reading aloud to others. This type of result should be examined further to understand some possible reasons why the student's reading motivation related to that subscale went down between the two survey administrations.

Class/Group-Level Analysis and Interpretation

The class/group-level results are an aggregate of the student level difference score data. The difference score results are used rather than the post-survey total scores, for example, because teachers are most likely interested in understanding the extent to which their class/group demonstrated growth in reading motivation (on average) rather than the average total score.

Before interpreting the mean, median, and standard deviation of the difference scores, however, it is important to understand how sample size (the number of students in the class/group) affects these sample statistics. The smaller the number of students in the analysis, the more one or two students with lower or higher difference scores relative to the other students in the class can skew the results.

For this reason, in most applications of the MMRP for teacher use, the median is likely to be a more accurate metric than the mean. Also, teachers will likely find that group-level analyses are less useful when there are only a few students in the group. Some teachers with less than 10 students, for example, may decide to not use the mean, median, or standard deviation at all as it does not add useful information to help them better serve the learning needs of their students.

Teachers administering the pre- and post-MMRP surveys to a larger number of students may find the group-level descriptive statistics (mean, median, and standard deviation) useful for helping them to understand which students have benefited more from the program than others. For example, the teacher could divide the class into low-, medium-, and high-growth groups and use that information alongside qualitative information about the program and student performance to discuss with colleagues why certain students appear to benefit more from the program in terms of reading motivation growth than others.

Interpreting the mean, median, and standard deviation of the difference scores requires knowledge of what those metrics mean and how they can be affected by sample size. The seven-student data set shown in Figures 8.1 and 8.2 will be used to illustrate how to accurately analyze and interpret these descriptive statistics.

The group *mean* in the example is 1.7 points. In other words, this group of seven students showed almost 2-point growth, on average, on the MMRP reading motivation survey from pre- to post-administration. The mean is the average across the student-level difference scores. Four of the seven students in the example showed positive growth between 2 to 6 points, one student had a negative difference score, and two students showed no growth.

The *median* can be used to signal the extent to which the mean either underestimates or overestimates the class or group's growth. In a normal distribution (i.e., think bell-shaped curve with more values toward the center and less as you move away), the mean and median are equal. The median is calculated by sorting from lowest to highest; the middle number in that sort is the median—in this case, 3 points of growth from pre to post.

If the median is greater than the mean, it signals that the mean *underestimates* the class/group's growth. Or, conversely, if the median is less than the mean, it signals that the mean *overestimates* the class or group's growth. In the running example used in this chapter (Figure 8.1), the teacher should use the median to interpret findings. These seven students showed positive growth around 3 points on the MMRP, in general, which is something to celebrate!

The final metric is the *standard deviation* of the difference scores for the class/group. A standard deviation is a measure of the amount of variability in the difference scores. Low standard deviation means data are clustered around the mean, and high standard deviation indicates difference scores are more spread out. Low and high are relative terms because standard deviations are always interpreted based on the amount of variability one might expect in the data range. The difference scores on the MMRP can range from +40 to -40 (80-point range) given that total scores can range from 20 to 60 points.

In our running example, difference scores range from -5 to +5 (10-point range), and the standard deviation is almost 4 points. When the standard deviation is larger than the mean or median, there is a lot of variability in the data. This is likely a reflection of the small sample size in this example. It simply indicates that the seven students do not have similar difference scores—their scores are very different! You can gather this information informally by examining Figure 8.2 and noticing that the bars in the graph are not all around the same height.

Overall, what might you infer about the group from the descriptive statistics (mean, median, and standard deviation) in Figure 8.1? Take a moment and jot down your thoughts. When you are ready, check your answer with the one provided below.

> Students overall tend to demonstrate about 3 points of growth on the MMRP reading motivation survey from pre- to post-administration, which is something to celebrate! However, there is a lot of variability around that midpoint given the size of the standard deviation, so it is important to examine individual student results.

How did you do? Was your interpretation similar to the one provided? Being able to calculate and interpret MMRP scores on both student and class levels can support your case studies of students' motivation by offering an indicator of how students' general motivation to read is progressing or not. If one or more students' MMRP scores decrease over time, or if one or more students' low scores do not improve, it may be time to take a closer look at how these students' motivation might be better supported.

Accurately calculating and interpreting MMRP scores can also assist you in offering specific feedback to students like Rocky (quoted at the start of this chapter) who are curious about how their motivation to read is progressing. If you do share with students about their MMRP scores, just make sure to share about their progress rather than their progress in comparison to others. Activity 8 will further support you in honing your skills. This time you will set up and input MMRP pre- and post-survey data in Excel before analyzing and interpreting findings.

SUMMARY

This chapter outlines suggested steps for analyzing and interpreting results from pre- and post-MMRP scores to support a case study of motivation. Step-by-step instructions are provided that show how an educator could use Excel to generate basic descriptive statistics at the student and class levels to better understand differences in students' pre- and post-MMRP scores. Explanations are provided about how the statistics should be properly interpreted and used to infer whether and how students' motivation to read differs over the period of time studied. The chapter ends with suggestions for using follow-up qualitative analyses to better understand the observed differences in students' scores at the student and/or class level.

Table 8.1. Activity 8: Completing Basic Analysis with Excel

Quantitative Analysis Exercises
Practice Exercise 1: Setting up and Inputting Data into Excel

Download the Excel template provided with this chapter or set up your own Excel spreadsheet using Figure 8.1 as a guide.

Input the following pre- and post-subscale scores for Jorge, Quincy, and Sara into Excel. Make sure to change the data range in the formulas for mean, median, and standard deviation!

Jorge
- Self-Concept: Pre=11; Post=11
- Value: Pre=24; Post=29
- Literacy Out loud: Pre=12; Post=18

Quincy
- Self-Concept: Pre=8; Post=8
- Value: Pre=18; Post=26
- Literacy Out loud: Pre=8; Post=14

Jorge
- Pre-Total MMRP Overall Score = _____
- Post-Total MMRP Overall Score = _____
- Difference between Pre/Post on SC Subscale = _____
- Difference between Pre/Post on V Subscale = _____
- Difference between Pre/Post on LO Subscale = _____
- Difference between Pre/Post on Total MMRP Overall Score = _____

Quincy
- Pre-Total MMRP Overall Score = _____
- Post-Total MMRP Overall Score = _____
- Difference between Pre/Post on SC Subscale = _____
- Difference between Pre/Post on V Subscale = _____
- Difference between Pre/Post on LO Subscale = _____
- Difference between Pre/Post on Total MMRP Overall Score = _____

Practice Exercise 1: Setting up and Inputting Data into Excel

Sara
- Self-Concept: Pre=13; Post=13
- Value: Pre=27; Post=31
- Literacy Out loud: Pre=10; Post=16

Calculate the total scores, difference scores between pre- and post-survey for the three subscales and overall, as well as the mean, median, and standard deviation of the difference scores. Add your answers in the right-hand column. See answer key below.

Sara
- Pre-Total MMRP Overall Score = _____
- Post-Total MMRP Overall Score = _____
- Difference between Pre/Post on SC Sub-scale = _____
- Difference between Pre/Post on V Sub-scale = _____
- Difference between Pre/Post on LO Sub-scale = _____
- Difference between Pre/Post on Total MMRP Overall Score = _____

Mean of Difference Scores: _____
Median of Difference Scores: _____
SD of Difference Scores: _____

Practice Exercise 2: Analyzing and Interpreting Results

Based upon the results from Practice Exercise 1, write your analysis and interpretation of the student-level and the group-level results in the right-hand column. See answer key below for a sample response guide.

Your Analysis and Interpretation
Student Level:
Group Level:

Practice Exercises Answer Key

Practice Exercise 1:

Jorge
Pre = 47
Post = 58
Difference between Pre/Post on SC = 0
Difference between Pre/Post on V = 5
Difference between Pre/Post on LO = 6
Difference between Pre/Post Total MMRP (Overall) = 11

Quincy
Pre = 34
Post = 48
Difference between Pre/Post on SC = 0
Difference between Pre/Post on V = 8
Difference between Pre/Post on LO = 6
Difference between Pre/Post Total MMRP (Overall) = 14

Sara
Pre = 50
Post = 60
Difference between Pre/Post on SC = 0
Difference between Pre/Post on V = 4
Difference between Pre/Post on LO = 6
Difference between Pre/Post Total MMRP (Overall) = 10
Mean = 11.7; Median = 11.0; Standard Deviation = 2.1

Practice Exercise 2:

Student-Level Analysis and Interpretation:
Jorge and Sara had similar pre- and post-survey total MMRP overall scores (47–50 points on the pre; and 58–60 on the post). Quincy had relatively low pre-survey responses (34 out of 60), signaling that most of his responses on the survey were 1's and 2's. Yet, Quincy also demonstrated more growth from pre- to post-survey than Jorge and Sara (14 points compared to 11 and 10, respectively). All three students demonstrated a lot of growth from pre- to post-survey as the difference scores were high (greater than or equal to 10).

However, from examining the subscale level difference scores, it is clear that all of the growth derives from the value and literacy out loud subscales; none of the three students showed growth on the self-concept subscale. This finding is something that I can look into further by engaging in one-on-one conversations with these three students about their responses to the self-concept items. This qualitative information will help me better understand their perceptions and how I could better support their growth in this critical area of reading motivation.

Group-Level Analysis and Interpretation:
There are three students in this data set. The three students' difference scores tended to cluster around the median/mean of 11 points of growth from pre- to post-survey—which is a significant amount of growth! The standard deviation is relatively small (about 2 points), which indicates that the three students tended to show similar amounts of growth to one another. The range was 10 to 14 points of growth.

REFERENCES

Marinak, B. A., Malloy, J. B., Gambrell, L. B., & Mazzoni, S. A. (2015). Me and my reading profile: A tool for assessing early reading motivation. *The Reading Teacher, 69*(1), 51–62. https://doi.org/10.1002/trtr.1362

Chapter 9

Presentations and Publications

Engaging Others in Your Work Inside and Outside of the Immediate Community

Joy Dangora Erickson and Cara E. Furman

> "Are you going to tell the principal what we said? Cause, I think you should."—Davy, age 6

Six-year-old Davy was excited to share during a walking-tour interview that he had an idea for how he might be able to read in a comfortable and quiet space during his reading intervention time. Davy reported that, if given the choice, he would opt to stay in his classroom instead of attending his reading intervention program. Though he recognized the importance of his group being together for instruction, he found that the noise level and hard chairs made it difficult for him to concentrate during independent reading time; the costs Davy associated with his participation appeared to outweigh the benefits.

Davy suggested that the school install sound-proof "pods" around the perimeter of the room in which kids could lie down and read in silence. He likened the pods to his favorite place to read at home—his top bunk bed. Though installing sound-proof reading pods may not be feasible, Davy's ideas about how his motivation for the intervention might be improved are supported by research: the noise level and the physical comfort of a room can enhance or impede one's willingness to read. Even if the school does not install Davy's pods, they may be able to do something else to decrease the noise and increase Davy's physical comfort in the reading space.

In asking the interviewer to pass his idea on to the principal, it is clear that Davy has some understanding of who has a large say in whether his ideas are actualized. Davy recognizes who holds the power in his community, and he is helping to democratize the decision-making process by requesting that his views be represented at the highest levels of the existing power structure. It is often in the best interests of you and your students to share anonymized case study findings with powerful stakeholders (e.g., principal, school board); they may be willing to help you change your program by offering various supports (e.g., financial, manual labor).

However, you need not stop there. There is good reason to also share what you have learned with people outside of your immediate school community. Just as completing your inquiry has made you think deeply about your practice, sharing your work can inspire others to do the same (Campbell, 2013; Cochran-Smith & Lytle, 2009; Dana & Yendol-Hoppey, 2020). This chapter discusses some potential benefits of sharing your findings inside and outside of your local community, and it offers ideas about how you might get started.

AN IMPORTANT REMINDER

As mentioned in other chapters (e.g., Chapter 2), it is important to remember that when you conduct case study work in your classroom or another's classroom with the intention of publishing from it, you must be mindful of Institutional Review Board (IRB) requirements. Even when classroom stories are shared anecdotally, permission from students and guardians are often required. If permission is granted, pseudonyms should replace participant and specific setting names. Protecting the identities of participants is imperative. If you are new to publishing and presenting, consult an experienced colleague to do right by your participants.

HOW WRITING UP AND SHARING YOUR WORK CAN BENEFIT YOU

Hopefully throughout this process you have had a few people to bounce ideas off of (e.g., a professor, an instructional coach, one or two peers) and to review your work. Better yet, you have worked closely with a small team of colleagues at key points in your process (e.g., data collection, data analysis) and have observed firsthand how your work is improved through collaboration. Perhaps a co-teacher or student teacher identified a better way or time to conduct student interviews. Maybe an instructional coach found something overlooked in the data. When it comes to conducting research, multiple heads are generally better than one.

Relatedly, writing up your project, a prerequisite for presenting and engaging others in it, can facilitate deep thinking and the remembering of important points, which may improve presentations as well as practice. You are forced to clarify and refine what you mean when you write (Cochran-Smith & Lytle, 2009; Mills, 2014; Paley, 1989). Not only must you be particular about the words that you select to describe key concepts and ideas, but you also must typically include and describe specific examples to support your ideas. There will be times when you learn or recall something new despite the hours you previously spent analyzing your data.

For example, when combing through the data a final time to add detailed examples to a final case report of three kindergarten children's motivation for their reading intervention, a teacher researcher realized that one child casually remarked in an interview that they did not have many books at home that they could read—most were too challenging. This piece of information did not directly connect to the research questions and so went largely unnoticed by the research team when completing the qualitative data analysis.

However, being familiar with the reading motivation literature and SEVT in particular (see Chapter 1), the teacher researcher knew that making sure the child had books at home they believed they could read was important for supporting motivation and skill acquisition. As such, she added a recommendation to the implications section of the report suggesting the team stock the child's home with books they were interested in and able to read. This addition gave the teacher researcher a sense of pride and accomplishment; she was able to better support her student and make another important contribution to the final report.

Writing and sharing your findings can empower you, the teacher, in important democratic ways. Many teachers are told what to teach and how to teach it; the scripted curricula mandated in many schools can rigidly limit teachers' autonomy by constraining their content and pedagogy (Fitz & Nikolaidis, 2020). Additionally, teachers are often forced to shoulder much of the blame when students are not making gains at the rate(s) others think they should be (Cochran-Smith et al., 2018). By studying and reflecting on your instruction in writing, you have hard evidence of your dedication and responsiveness to individual students.

Armed with that evidence, you are able to challenge recommendations and/or mandates made by others that you believe do not meet the needs of your specific students in your specific context (Campbell, 2013; Cochran-Smith & Lytle, 2009). If you choose to publish and/or present your findings outside of your school community, you can advocate not only for your own students but also for other children.

Finally, teaching can be lonely work. You may have already known that it is crucial to support children's reading motivation; however, working in isolation, you might have questioned yourself. Conducting case studies with a team and sharing your findings with others can confirm what you knew and help you identify blind spots. Writing and sharing your work can be particularly affirming. More on how to present and/or publish your work inside and outside of your school community is offered in later sections of this chapter.

HOW YOUR WORK CAN BENEFIT STUDENTS

Some of the ways students stand to benefit from you writing and sharing your work are fairly obvious. For example, formally articulating your findings and their implications for practice in print can encourage you to follow through on making changes to your program. These changes, informed in part by students' own motivation-related perceptions, should lead to improved motivation and engagement in students. Improved motivation and engagement can support students' rate of skill acquisition and achievement.

Of course, you will need to monitor students' progress in these areas to determine the degree to which the altered program is effective. You might add this follow-up information to your written report at a later date or conduct a new study. Your regular monitoring and support of students' motivation and achievement can result in their enjoyment and valuing of school-based reading experiences as well as their meeting important academic benchmarks—two vitally important outcomes.

Another potential benefit of writing about your work is the empowerment of students. Anti-oppression scholar and reformer Lisa Delpit (2001), among others, has long underscored that students should have a say in what and how things are done in their classrooms and schools: "The teacher cannot be the only expert in the classroom. To deny students their own expert knowledge is to disempower them" (p. 288). Amplifying students' voices can function to democratize research and instruction by permitting students some representation in the existing power structure(s) (Cochran-Smith et al., 2018).

Recall the enthusiasm with which Davy asked that his idea be shared with the principal. Imagine his excitement if the school enacted his vision of learning pods or something like them rooted in his feedback. Agreeing to bring Davy's idea to the decision-making table can help Davy see himself as a contributing member of his community. He may feel empowered to more regularly share his opinions and ideas, which may lead to improved learning outcomes, contribute to his sense of self, and promote a more democratic approach to making decisions that directly impacts students.

HOW YOUR WORK CAN BENEFIT COLLEAGUES

Given the intense national focus on reading skill acquisition and academic achievement, it is not a stretch to assume that reading motivation is not at the forefront of teachers' minds. By communicating what you have learned about reading motivation and your students' motivation to your colleagues, you can introduce them to or remind them of the relationship between motivation and skill acquisition. You may also inspire them to conduct their own research. Oftentimes, the colleagues you collaborate with through your study gain confidence in their own abilities to complete a research project.

This trend is in part what brought this text to life. Teachers, reading specialists, instructional coaches, and school administrators involved in some of the reading motivation research projects referenced throughout this text requested a handbook they could consult to jumpstart and/or guide their own explorations of young children's motivation for reading programs. Similarly, university and college teacher preparation professors shared that the preservice and inservice teachers they worked with would appreciate having an accessible reference when completing research projects centered on children's motivation.

When your colleagues carry out their own projects, their professional knowledge grows. They learn not only about motivation and how it shapes skill acquisition and achievement but also about research—namely, how it is conducted and interpreted. These valuable skills can support them when reviewing education journals, attending professional meetings, and participating in professional trainings. They also learn about their students. Most educators care about their students' perceptions of their instruction; conducting a case study of motivation encourages them to make time for eliciting students' views and take them seriously.

HOW YOUR WORK CAN BENEFIT OTHERS OUTSIDE YOUR SCHOOL COMMUNITY

Your work can inspire others outside of your school community to examine young children's motivation for reading programs too. When you present at conferences and/or publish in professional journals, you stand to push the thinking of your attendees and readers in new directions. These may be school leaders who, after engaging with your work, encourage their faculty and staff to take a closer look at students' reading motivation. Or they may be researchers who decide that your study warrants paying closer attention to young children's reading motivation on a larger scale.

Either way, your work has provoked thought in the minds of people outside of your school community, which could have a wider reaching impact on practice and even research and theory. More young children may be asked about their motivation for reading programs. Children's own voices might begin to be better represented in existing power structures, and research designs and instructional decisions might be more inclusive of children's views. Presenting and publishing is not for everyone; however, teachers who are willing to do one or both may improve more children's school reading experiences than they thought possible.

HOW MIGHT YOU SHARE YOUR RESEARCH WITH COLLEAGUES?

Something to consider when deciding how to share your work with colleagues is the role you want them to play. Are they audience members, participants, co-collaborators? This depends on both the kind of information you have to share as well as the way you envision your colleagues engaging with your work. For example, suppose a second-grade teacher conducted a case study of her students' motivation for their daily reading routines and discovered that many appeared to have low motivation for the spelling portion of instruction.

In response to these findings, she did some additional research on how she might better engage children in spelling routines. Combining (1) the knowledge she gained from reviewing the reading motivation literature at the start of the study, (2) what she learned from interviewing and observing her students throughout the study, and (3) the additional research on spelling she collected at the end, the teacher created some new spelling resources and tried them out with her class. She then repeated the inquiry cycle, following up with students to infer whether their motivation and engagement was improving with the new approach.

With the support of research team members, she wrote her process and findings up in the form of a research (i.e., case) report to clarify what she might share with different audiences. The report included several sections: (1) an introduction explaining why the study was conducted and what was already known about the topic, (2) a methods section explaining what she and the team did during each phase of the project, (3) a results section consisting of major findings, and (4) a discussion section connecting findings to the motivation literature and posing new questions. For detailed information on how to write a research report, see Hancock and Algozzine (2011).

Depending on which aspect(s) of her work she chooses to share, she may draw on a range of formats—possibly even combining a few. For example, to share her review of the research on motivation including relevant theories and promising practices, she may create a brief slideshow in Google Slides or PowerPoint that offers important highlights from this sea of information. If she selects this presentation option, she should keep each slide simple (i.e., use text sparingly), pair important concepts with images, and ensure charts are readable by using an appropriately sized font.

The teacher's slides could also be distributed to audience members in the form of an electronic or hardcopy handout. Alternatively, teachers may prefer offering a one-page bulleted handout or a flyer with visuals and short paragraphs.

If a main goal of the slide presentation is to highlight the ways in which ideas, concepts, and/or findings are related, Prezi can be a useful tool. It allows the user to pan out and zoom in on points and images that may support your audience's attention. If the teacher aims to give her colleagues access to multiple important resources such as articles, games, materials, videos of children trying out activities, and/or her presentation handouts, Padlet might best support the organization and distribution of her materials.

Maybe the teacher seeks a more interactive experience; she aims for her colleagues to participate in her presentation. Her review of the literature and her students' self-reports suggested they might benefit motivationally and academically from playfully discriminating between, practicing, and reflecting on spelling patterns in a systematic and hands-on way. Therefore, she investigated, selected, and implemented multiple spelling games that appear to be more supportive for her students' motivation and skill acquisition.

In this case, she might set up a series of centers showcasing each new game and affording her colleagues an opportunity to experience each one. They might then reassemble together in another space to share out in rounds what they took away from the experience and how they might use each resource in their own classrooms. This kind of interactive presentation can involve everyone and promote a collaborative approach to learning.

Alternatively, the teacher might hope her colleagues can help her solve a problem encountered during the research process. Practitioner Inquiry Groups (PIGs), another potential sharing approach capable of involving everyone and facilitating collaborative meaning making, generally center on a question. The question can either be posed by an individual (e.g., the teacher) or generated by the group after reviewing a portion of the teacher's collected data (Kroll & Meier, 2018).

Professional Learning Communities (PLCs) similarly pool the knowledge of a group. Knowing from her research that children are motivated by a broad range of resources and that a diverse offering can benefit many children, perhaps the teacher asks everyone to come to the group with a favorite spelling game or material they use in their classroom. She opens her presentation by sharing research on inclusion in a slideshow presentation. Then, she invites everyone to share their favorite game.

One approach that is sure to get everyone involved and give people a chance to interact with each other and the materials is "speed dating." In this activity, teachers are given a short window of time (5 minutes or so) to teach each other how to play their game. When the time is up, they move on to the next person. Sitting in a configuration that includes an inner circle and an outer circle ensures everyone gets a chance to participate.

HOW MIGHT YOU SHARE YOUR RESEARCH WITH THOSE OUTSIDE YOUR SCHOOL SETTING?

At the beginning of this chapter, Davy knew that his personal experience made him an authority. He extrapolated from his preferred reading spot at home, the top of his bunk bed, that other children might like to read in similar, quiet, "pods." In doing so, Davy drew on the particular and mined it for themes (the value of quiet, cozy, and separate) from which one might generalize. This is also what teacher researchers do. They draw on data typically collected in their classroom or school, support it with external sources, and analyze it for themes.

Countless organizations provide spaces for teachers to gather, share their work, and learn together. For example, the North Dakota Study Group on evaluation hosts a yearly gathering specifically for teachers. Similarly, the National Writing Project hosts satellite projects across the country aimed at bringing teachers together to write and study. And the Summer Institute on Descriptive Inquiry supports teachers seeking to use descriptive observation to study children and children's works.

Annual conferences hosted by national and international professional organizations offer additional outlets for sharing your work. These include the International Literacy Association (ILA), the Literacy Research Association (LRA), and the National Council of Teachers of English (NCTE). Many state or regional professional organizations also put on annual conferences (e.g., the Massachusetts Reading Association [MRA], the Progressive Education Network [PEN]).

Some teachers appreciate the energy and exchange of ideas that conferences afford. An oral presentation can play to teachers' strengths, as communicating in front of a group is a skill classroom teachers practice every day. Learning with other passionate colleagues can be revitalizing. For detailed information on how to prepare for conference presentations, see Dana & Yendol-Hoppey (2020).

Many literacy teachers are also confident and passionate writers. Writing can be enjoyable for teachers because it often requires skills different from those needed for daily teaching duties. It can be an opportunity to share ideas with people across time and space. Your writing may also reach a wider audience.

Personal blogs can be a great place to share writing related to your study. Educator blogs published by Edutopia and TeachThought provide spaces for teachers to share their stories. Professional journals including *The Reading Teacher*, *Journal of Practitioner Research*, and *Networks: An Online Journal for Teacher Research* welcome teacher writing and are geared toward a teacher readership.

Other journals such as Bank Street's *Occasional Papers*, *Schools: Studies in Education*, and the *Voice of Practitioners* section of *Young Children* aim to reach teacher and researcher audiences. In doing so, they afford an additional advocacy opportunity by encouraging teachers to speak back to researchers. When teachers publish in these outlets, they bring their voices, experiences, and knowledge of students like Davy as well as their own expertise to the table.

SUMMARY

Teacher researchers capitalize on inquiry, observation, and analysis to make improvements in their classroom. When they share this research with colleagues, they can make changes in their school communities. The ripple effect widens when they present their work to a wider public. This chapter began with Davy's desire to be seen and heard by his principal. Davy knew he had something important to share.

Like Davy, when teachers share their research, it stands to benefit them: helping them to make sense of and sort through what they've learned. It can be empowering and energizing. Teacher research benefits colleagues—expanding what they know as teachers and motivating them to also look at challenges in their classrooms as opportunities to learn. Sharing research outside one's school community benefits the field. Doing so gives teachers the chance to showcase what they know, contribute to a greater knowledge base, and get feedback.

Teachers learn from each other as they share ideas. Traditional researchers benefit from hearing what happens on the ground in classrooms. There are many ways to share one's work. When considering how to share, it is important to consider the goals of the presentation. Considering the presentation's goals will help you determine the medium and the method. When choosing a venue, it is important to think about the audience you aim to reach as well as your preferred medium of communication.

Table 9.1. Activity 9

Case Study Write-up and Presentation Planning Exercise	
Use your completed activities from Chapters 1–8, any other relevant resources (e.g., your memos) along with this chart to: • write up your study • think carefully about what you might present, to whom you might present it, and the format you might use.	Figure 9.1. *James Dangora* 
1. **Title of Study:**	
2. **Introduction:** • Explain why you conducted the study (i.e., share your rationale). • Support your rationale with important information (e.g., findings, theories) from the reading motivation literature. • State your main goals (aims) for the study (i.e., what you intend to accomplish). • State your specific research question(s).	*Do you intend to share this information?* **Yes No** With whom might you share it? Why? Which presentation format(s) might you use? Why?
3. **Methods:** • Describe your setting. • Describe your participants (i.e., the people who participated in the project). • List the types of data you collected and explain why you selected each type. • Summarize your data collection schedule and the procedures you followed to collect your data. • Explain how you analyzed the data.	*Do you intend to share this information?* **Yes No** With whom might you share it? Why? Which presentation format(s) might you use? Why?

4. **Results:** • Summarize your major finding(s) (e.g., themes) in relation to each research question(s). • Report any exceptions to these major findings. • Report anything that surprised you. • If studying a small group of children, consider organizing and summarizing important findings by child.	*Do you intend to share this information?* **Yes No** With whom might you share it? Why? Which presentation format(s) might you use? Why?
5. **Discussion:** • Tie what you found to what is written in the scholarly motivation literature. What makes sense in reference to the literature? What does not? Why might this be? • Discuss the implications of this study. What might findings mean for you as a teacher? For your students? For reading instruction and/or schooling in general? • Are you left with new questions? List them and explain what you and others might do to begin answering them.	*Do you intend to share this information?* **Yes No** With whom might you share it? Why? Which presentation format(s) might you use? Why?

REFERENCES

Campbell, K. H. (2013). A call to action: Why we need more practitioner research. *Democracy & Education, 21*(2), 1–8.

Cochran-Smith, M., Carney, M. C., Keefe, E. S., Burton, S., Chang, W., Fernández, M. B., Miller, A., Sánchez, J. G., & Baker, M. (2018). *Reclaiming accountability in teacher education.* Teachers College Press.

Cochran-Smith, M., & Lytle, S. L. (2009). *Inquiry as stance: Practitioner research for the next generation.* Teachers College Press.

Dana, N. F., & Yendol-Hoppey, D. (2020). *The reflective educator's guide to classroom research: Learning to teach and teaching to learn through practitioner inquiry* (4th ed.). Corwin.

Delpit, L. D. (2001). The silenced dialogue: Power and pedagogy in educating other people's children. In K. Halasek & N. P. Highberg (Eds.), *Landmark essays on basic writing* (pp. 83–101). Hermagoras Press.

Fitz, J. A., & Nikolaidis, A. C. (2020). A democratic critique of scripted curriculum. *Journal of Curriculum Studies, 52*(2), 195–213. https://doi.org/10.1080/00220272.2019.1661524

Hancock, D. R., & Algozzine, B. (2011). *Doing case study research: A practical guide for beginning researchers* (2nd ed.). Teachers College Press.

Kroll, L. R., & Meier, D. R. (2018). *Documentation and inquiry in the early childhood classroom: Research stories from urban centers and schools.* Routledge.

Mills, G. E. (2014). *Action research: A guide for the teacher researcher* (5th ed.). Pearson.

Paley, V. (1989). *Must teachers also be writers?* Occasional Paper No. 13. Center for the Study of Writing.

Chapter 10

Tweaking Your Practice, Documenting What Happens, and Beginning Again

Joy Dangora Erickson and Alessandra E. Ward

"These [books] are so much more better."—Hope, age 5

In response to findings from a case study of her students' motivation for a specific reading intervention program, Hope's teacher sought out and replaced several students' previous decodable texts with ones the students were more interested in reading. For Hope, this seemed to make all the difference. Hope's teacher reported that she appeared more engaged in her independent reading a month after the book swap, and Hope reported that she wanted to come to the intervention room primarily to read the new books.

However, the new texts matched to students' interests were not enough to motivate another member of the intervention group. Trent continued to report low motivation and appear disengaged despite the integration of new dinosaur-themed texts. Hope and Trent's teacher wondered, "Why aren't my changes working for Trent?" Two interviews and several observations later, the teacher and her research team confirmed that even though Trent was interested in the new books, he believed they were too difficult to read independently.

Due to her familiarity with the motivation literature and SEVT specifically (See Chapter 1), Trent's teacher knew that the degree to which Trent perceived himself able to read the texts was likely to influence his motivation. With the reading specialist, she created a decodable dinosaur text that better reflected what Trent believed he could do on his own. This text served as a bridge connecting Trent to the more challenging texts, which he confidently began reading soon thereafter. Once Trent and his teacher agreed the intervention was working for him, a third student's motivation became a concern.

Niko appreciated the robot-themed texts his teacher provided but still slumped in his seat upon arrival and appeared reluctant to work with his group members. The only time during the intervention he seemed sufficiently engaged was during independent reading practice when he was reading the robot books. This time, the teacher wondered, "What's not working for Niko?" Again, working closely with her team, the teacher discovered that Niko struggled with leaving his classroom and his good friend behind to attend the reading intervention.

Niko very much enjoyed reading the robot-themed books; however, he wanted to remain in his classroom where he could share them with his friend. He also wondered what his friend was doing in the classroom while he was attending intervention. Niko was afraid that he was missing out on activities he believed were more fun. In sum, he attributed a high opportunity cost to his participation in the intervention, and it was impeding his motivation to work there. Niko's case proved more complex than both Hope's and Trent's and resulted in Niko and his teacher coming up with a compromise.

To ensure Niko was getting the targeted reading instruction he needed in a quiet space, he would continue to attend the intervention four times per week. However, once a week his teacher agreed to bring the boys together to share what each was doing during the time Niko attended the intervention. When they connected, they could take turns reading their independent reading books to one another and discuss them. Other times, Niko's friend would be invited to participate in the intervention, and Niko could attend his friend's small group reading session. Niko's teacher would continue to inquire about his motivation and the motivation of others.

A main takeaway from this anecdote is the importance of making changes to your practice based on findings from your systematic inquiry and following up to see if those changes are having the desired effect(s). Put differently, teachers are wise to adopt what Cochran-Smith and Lytle (1999, 2009) refer to as an *inquiry stance* toward teaching and researching. Such a position when interpreted specifically in relation to reading instruction suggests you should regularly examine your students' motivation for school programming and adjust it just as you do for their developing reading skills.

In the sections that follow, an inquiry stance approach to teaching and learning is discussed in greater detail. Additionally, a set of tips for how you might work toward adopting and maintaining an inquiry stance throughout your career is offered.

ADOPTING AN INQUIRY STANCE

This book has put forth a rationale and method for examining children's motivation to participate in their reading programs. Hopefully, completing your first research project has helped you realize how inquiring about students' views of programming can support your teaching and their learning and inspired you to keep asking questions and systematically examining them. The completion of your first project is an important step toward adopting a broader inquiry stance toward your practice.

According to Cochran-Smith and Lytle (2009), "Inquiry is a critical habit of mind that informs professional work in all aspects" (p.121). Asking questions about how a specific reading program is shaping students' motivation to participate and reflecting deeply and critically on the data you collected to answer those questions has likely left you with more questions. Some questions may resemble those you previously asked (e.g., Why might student X be demonstrating low motivation for this program?). As the chapter's opening vignette illustrates, it is important to regularly monitor students' motivation and make adjustments as needed.

However, other questions worth exploring may relate to issues of access, equity, and power. For example, you may now be wondering why the reading program and/or your administration requires students to read certain books and why you or someone else (e.g., reading interventionist) has been told they must maintain fidelity to a program that does not appear to be working for some students.

Recall that in the chapter's opening vignette three students each wanted to read about a different topic. The teacher's freedom to offer the students books they are interested in seems imperative to their equitable access to reading practice and, in turn, their success. Questions of what to do, how to do it, and who gets to decide are at the heart of taking an inquiry stance (Cochran-Smith and Lytle, 2009). Put differently, while you should regularly examine all students' motivation for their reading programs for the reasons emphasized throughout this text, taking an inquiry stance also necessitates formulating wonderings about educational equity.

Cochran-Smith and Lytle (2009) underscore that assuming an inquiry stance

> involves a continual process of making current arrangements problematic; questioning the ways knowledge and practice are constructed, evaluated, and used; and assuming that part of the work of practitioners individually and collectively is to participate in educational and social change. (p. 121)

Research, teaching, and activism work in tandem when taking an inquiry stance. Practitioner research is unending; good teachers engage in research throughout their careers to improve instruction, enhance learning, and advocate for the well-being of students.

Filtered through an inquiry stance lens, the major steps involved in completing a case study of students' motivation as described in the chapters preceding this one include the following:

- Deciding on one or more inquiry questions
- Examining the scholarly literature to familiarize yourself with what is already known about your topic
- Collecting the data you need to answer your inquiry question(s)
- Systematically analyzing your data as you collect it (i.e., formatively) and afterward (i.e., summatively)
- Writing a report of your findings and making decisions about which aspects of your work you would like to share, with whom, and how
- Changing your practice and/or the program as needed in alignment with your findings
- Asking more questions (e.g., Are my changes working?; Is this program equitable?)
- Repeating this process

Some teacher researchers have multiple research projects going on at the same time. It is not uncommon, for example, to be sharing what you learned from one project while you collect data for another.

It is also not uncommon when embodying an inquiry stance to dig deeper into potential issues of equity that capture your attention as a result of your study/studies. For example, if you have good reason to suspect that an alternate reading program, maybe even one offered outside of your community, is a better fit in terms of building foundational reading skills and supporting motivation, you might wonder whether one or more children should have access to that program and how they might gain it.

If you are new to conducting classroom research, thinking about your next project and/or identifying and acting upon opportunities for advancing educational equity might feel overwhelming. That is ok—this is a lifelong professional journey. Consider starting small: complete a rigorous case study of one or more students' motivation using the process described in this text and choose just one or two of the following tips to consider. Then, repeat the process, deepening your equity work and broadening your inquiry a little more each time.

FIVE TIPS FOR TAKING AN INQUIRY STANCE

The late Loris Malaguzzi, psychologist and founder of the Reggio Emilia philosophy of early childhood education, is credited with establishing a democratic, child-centered, and community-oriented network of early learning centers in Italy. Malaguzzi's philosophy and the network of Reggio schools more generally have historically served as a model for early childhood education around the world. At the heart of this approach is a continuous cycle of inquiry. Reggio educators embody an inquiry stance (Reggio Children, 2020); they relentlessly question the status quo and interrogate their practice to improve teaching, learning, and society.

According to Malaguzzi,

> [Teachers] need to know that it is possible to engage in the challenge of longitudinal observations and small research projects concerning the development and experiences of children. Indeed, education without research or innovation is education without interest. (Malaguzzi as cited in Gandini, 2012, p. 49).

To meet the needs of individual learners, Reggio teachers study them intensely and intentionally. The five tips offered below were inspired by some of Malaguzzi's most memorable comments on the relationship between research and good teaching.

1. Keep up on Current Research

> *"We have no alternatives but continuous professional development"* (*Malaguzzi* as cited in Gandini, 2012, p. *48).*

The importance of keeping abreast of research findings specific to teaching and learning cannot be overstated. This text has offered a concise synthesis of findings from a selection of impactful empirical studies focused on reading motivation (see Chapter 3); however, new studies are published all the time. How might you continue to build your professional knowledge as a means of questioning your practice?

Professional organizations can be excellent places to start. The International Literacy Association (ILA), for example, regularly shares pertinent findings from new studies specific to literacy, and including reading motivation, in a variety of ways. We encourage you to join the organization and gain access to their professional journals. Without a membership you can access the ILA blog, *Literacy Now* (https://www.literacyworldwide.org/blog).

Other large-scale professional organizations you might consider include the American Psychological Association (APA), the Literacy Research Association (LRA), and the National Council of Teachers of English (NCTE). Smaller state and regional organizations (e.g., the Massachusetts Reading Association [MRA]) also offer members valuable resources in a variety of formats (e.g., journals, newsletters).

In addition to offering a wealth of information online and in the mail, professional organizations afford opportunities to learn through in-person and/or virtual events. Conferences, book clubs, and webinars are just a few of the ways professional organizations communicate new research findings to members. Finally, nearly all professional organizations have social media accounts (e.g., Twitter, Facebook). Follow these organizations to learn of major findings from new research, which are blasted out often.

2. Listen to and Observe Your Students Often

> *"To learn and relearn together with the children is our line of work"* (Malaguzzi as cited in Gandini, 2012, p. 61).

How children experience schooling matters; their perceptions of that which occurs in school may impact their motivation to participate more than objective reality itself (assuming one exists). And the degree to which they actively participate in lessons influences how much progress they make. Therefore, it is imperative that trusted adults inquire about and take seriously how children are experiencing school programming. Children's own insights may lead to improvements in teaching and learning, which in turn, can yield more equitable outcomes.

As has been emphasized throughout this text, the ways teacher researchers go about eliciting young children's motivation-related perceptions also matters. Children should be invited by trusted adults to share their views in nonthreatening ways that make sense to them. Conversational drawing interviews and walking-tour interviews are two methods referenced in this text (see Chapter 4). For information on other successful interview approaches, see O'Reilly and Dogra's *Interviewing Children and Young People for Research* (2017) and Clark and Moss's *Listening to Young Children: The Mosaic Approach* (2011).

Careful observation of children in their learning environment(s) can also support teacher researchers in better understanding how children experience school. Recall that engagement is an expression of children's motivation for a task or activity. Field notes and reflective journals are two ways teacher researchers can record and reflect on observations of students' engagement (see Chapter 4). However, many different child observation techniques exist. For more information on conducting observations of young children in teacher-directed activities, see Cohen and colleagues' *Observing and Recording the Behavior of Young Children* (2015).

When it comes to examining children's engagement, it can be difficult to know for sure how actively engaged they really are. Engagement consists of three dimensions (i.e., cognitive, emotional, and behavioral), and the best way to determine an individual's level of engagement is to consider all three (for a more detailed explanation of how engagement is conceptualized, see Davis et al., 2012; Center for Innovation in Teaching and Learning, 2020). Yet, indicators of behavioral engagement (e.g., time on task) are what many focus on during observations because they are more readily observable.

When primarily examining behavioral engagement, teacher researchers can misinterpret behaviors. For example, compliance may be mistaken for high engagement while other behaviors (e.g., fidgeting) may be misinterpreted for low engagement. This is not to say teachers should ignore children's behaviors during lessons; they should pay careful attention to children's behaviors and interpret them in conjunction with other information including children's own self-reports.

3. Solicit Feedback from Many

> *"[The Reggio Approach] invites an exchange of ideas, it has an open and democratic style, and it tends to open minds"* (Malaguzzi as cited in Gandini, 2012, p. 43).

Everyone comes to teaching and research with blind spots; experiences and deep-seated beliefs, values, and biases, among other factors, color how each person perceives what they pay attention to and how they interpret information. No matter how objective one tries to be, they cannot help but view the world through their individual lens. It is for this reason that multiple perspectives should be considered when planning for instruction and doing classroom research. This text has repeatedly advocated for working with a team.

If you are just beginning to do research in your classroom, your team might be quite small. Perhaps it consists only of you, a trusted mentor (e.g., professor, instructional coach) or colleague, and the children. With experience you will become more comfortable with ongoing inquiry and the research process itself; feeling more in control, you may be inclined to open up your work to additional scrutiny from others.

As explained in previous chapters (e.g., Chapter 5, Chapter 7), involving others in your inquiries can have many benefits. Specifically, it can make the research process more manageable and enjoyable, increase the trustworthiness of conclusions, and spark new ideas. Additionally, adding team members to your practitioner-research network can support you in bringing about positive change on a larger scale.

The people who work with you may be inspired to launch their own inquiry projects that lead to improved instruction and student outcomes. They may try out one or more of the changes you made to your practice and find it to be successful in their setting. Or they may begin to ask more questions about access and equity. Any one of these outcomes may lead to serious educational improvements for children. In sum, increasing the number of people involved in your inquiry work can improve your projects and widen your views while opening others' minds to inquiry as stance.

4. Reflect on and Interrogate Your Practice Informally and Formally:

> *"Teachers—like children and everyone else—feel the need to grow in their competences; they want to transform experiences into thoughts, thoughts into reflections, the reflections into new thoughts and new actions"* (*Malaguzzi as cited in Gandini, 2012*, p. 48).

A great way to do this, as stated previously, is to keep a reflective journal. Reviewing your past and ongoing reflections is a crucial support for data analysis and interpretation, as well as making positive changes to your practice as a result of your analysis. Reflecting through conversation (oral or written, in person or virtual) with a trusted colleague can take this a step further and reveal issues and/or insights you may have missed. Consider a shared Google doc as a journal or call a colleague on your drive home and use the commute as a reflective period.

Open-ended reflections, in which you write or speak to whatever comes up at the time, are an excellent tool. However, you may wish to complement these with some more structured reflections in response to questions or prompts. You can generate a list in advance (colleagues can help with this) and then use the list as a springboard for deepening your thinking. Structured prompts can also help you interrogate areas of your practice that you might be more likely to miss, such as issues of access and equity. See Tip 5 for a list of potential prompts and questions to get you started in reflecting through an equity lens.

5. Ask Questions About Access and Equity

> *"The wider the range of possibilities we offer children, the more intense will be their motivation and the richer their experiences"* (Malaguzzi as cited in Gandini, 2012, p.48).

The only way to make your practice more equitable is to accept that we are all participants in an educational system that continues to oppress certain groups; some students have historically been and continue to benefit from the system more than others. All teachers have routines and practices that unintentionally exclude some students and/or make them feel as if they do not belong.

The good news is that you can influence the system by starting with your own classroom. Conducting case studies of children's motivation for the programs you offer is one powerful way to better understand who has access to effective programming and who does not. However, there are other ways to see what you missed previously that may make your classroom a more inclusive space. Here are a few reflection questions, many tailored specifically to the literacy intervention setting, that you can use to support you on this journey:

- How did I support students' equitable participation in this lesson/activity? How did I offer avenues for students who may be less comfortable communicating orally to share their ideas?
- How have I been sensitive to differences of language and dialect in this lesson/activity? Have I communicated possibly to any students that their way of speaking is wrong or inappropriate (for example, by correcting a student who said, "I be goin'" when this is appropriate in their community)? If so, how can I make amends?
- How have I been responsive to students' varied interests and cultural practices in this lesson/activity? Which texts have I included? Who could see themselves in these texts, and who might not have been able to?
- What messages may I have communicated in this lesson/activity about the value of students' home literacy practices, especially if those were considered in comparison to schooled literacy practices?
- What opportunities for student voice, choice, and agency have I offered in this lesson/activity? How can I incorporate more of these opportunities?
- In what ways have I honored students as experts in this lesson/activity? How have I supported my students to see themselves as more than simply students who need extra support?

- How have I made it possible for all students to share their honest opinions of my instruction, without fear of reprisal? How have I created a safe space to amplify their voices?

Perhaps you have already been doing some of the actions described in these five tips and completing your first case study has compelled you to try one or two more. Perhaps you are celebrating seeing through your first study from start to finish and need some time to recuperate. Wherever you currently find yourself, continue to work toward the goal of embodying an inquiry stance. You will find that by doing so, you improve your practice and increase your students' opportunities for success.

SUMMARY

This chapter opens by highlighting some changes one teacher made to her practice in response to her case study findings, including bringing in additional texts aligned with students' interests, providing decodable texts that could serve as a bridge to more complex text and therefore support students' self-efficacy, and offering opportunities for social collaboration both inside and outside the intervention space.

The chapter then offers tips for how to adopt an inquiry stance, or "critical habit of mind" (Cochran-Smith & Lytle, 2009, p. 121). In addition to asking

Table 10.1. Activity 10

Where Might You Go Next? Instructional Planning Exercise	
Review each profile generated from a case study of the students' motivation for their reading intervention program. Then think about what you might do to better support each student's motivation and engagement within and potentially beyond the program using the prompts provided.	Figure 10.1. *James Dangora* 

Profile A	Profile B	Profile C
Kindergarten student Janice reported on several occasions that she gets nervous before doing letter-sound drills during her reading intervention. Despite liking the other two major components of the intervention (i.e., word building and independent reading), she shared that, if given the choice, she would not go to the intervention because of the drills. Careful observations of Janice support her view. Specifically, she struggles with the drill while the other members of her group answer with relative ease. Occasionally, Janice has been observed to shut down during or soon after the drill.	Kindergarten student Gunner reports that he largely enjoys attending the reading intervention but that he misses several peers who remain in the classroom when he leaves for the intervention room. He regularly expresses concern to the interventionist that he is missing time with his peers and that he is missing what he perceives to be exciting happenings in the classroom. Additionally, he shares in multiple interviews with another member of the research team that he would really like to show his friends in the classroom that he can read. Observations reveal that Gunner has been more reluctant than usual to leave the classroom and eager to leave the intervention early. The most recent observations also suggest that he is speeding through his independent reading time at the end of the intervention to line up at the door in hopes of returning to his classroom sooner.	Kindergarten student Amelia is bilingual and is learning to read in Portuguese at the same time she is learning to read in English. She reveals in an interview that she much prefers reading at home with various members of her family to reading in the intervention setting; she maintains that she would not go to the intervention if she had the choice. Specifically, Amelia likes sitting in her avó's lap with a blanket while they take turns reading the pages of her favorite Portuguese storybook. Amelia also shares that she does not like participating in intervention letter-sound drills because she gets confused about whether she is supposed to say the English sound(s) associated with the letter(s) or the Portuguese sound(s). Remembering the sounds associated with the letter h in each language, for example, is especially challenging for her. Amelia's hesitation to participate in letter sound-drills has been observed several times.

What changes to the intervention program might you consider to better support each student's motivation?

> What other questions might you explore either formally (i.e., with another study) or informally about the group and/or about each individual in an effort to gain them and/or others equitable access to programming that more holistically meets their needs?

questions about motivation, an inquiry stance requires probing issues of educational equity. Tips for taking an inquiry stance include the following: (1) keep up on current research, (2) listen to and observe your students often, (3) solicit feedback from many, (4) reflect on and interrogate your practice formally and informally, and (5) ask questions about access and equity. Specific reflection questions are provided to support your reflection on important issues of equity as they relate to literacy motivation.

REFERENCES

Clark, A., & Moss, P. (2011). *Listening to young children: The mosaic approach* (2nd ed.). National Children's Bureau.

Cochran-Smith, M., & Lytle, S. L. (1999). The teacher research movement: A decade later. *Educational Researcher, 28*(7), 15–25.

Cochran-Smith, M., & Lytle, S. L. (2009). *Inquiry as stance: Practitioner research for the next generation.* Teachers College Press.

Cohen, D. H., Stern, V., Balaban, N., & Gropper, N. (2015). *Observing and recording the behavior of young children* (6th ed.). Teachers College Press.

Davis, H. A., Summers, J. J., & Miller, L. M. (2012). What does it mean for students to be engaged? In H. A. Davis, J. J. Summers, & L. M. Miller (Eds.), *An interpersonal approach to classroom management: Strategies for improving student engagement* (pp. 21–33). Corwin Press.

Gandini, L. (2012). History, ideas, and basic principles: An interview with Loris Malaguzzi. In C. Edwards, L. Gandini, & G. Forman (Eds.), *The hundred languages of children: The Reggio Emilia experience in transformation* (3rd ed., pp. 27–71). Praeger.

Reggio Children. (2020). *Loris Malaguzzi.* https://www.reggiochildren.it/en/reggio-emilia-approach/loris-malaguzzi/

O'Reilly, M., & Dogra, N. (2017). *Interviewing children and young people for research.* Sage.

Center for Innovation in Teaching and Learning. (2020, September 15). *Three dimensions of student engagement.* https://citl.illinois.edu/citl-101/teaching-learning/resources/teaching-across-modalities/teaching-tips-articles/teaching-tips/2020/09/15/three-dimensions-of-student-engagement

Epilogue

Joy Dangora Erickson and Cara E. Furman

"By utilizing the most reliable information we can gather to inform and shape our teacher research, we can justify our claims that we are constantly improving our practices so we can provide the best *experiences* possible for the children we teach."—(Hatch, 2012, p.ix; emphasis added)

Recall that this quote opened the preface of this text. It was used to underscore the need to investigate children's motivation for their reading programs in order to better support their motivation and engagement within these programs. Maximizing children's motivation for and engagement in their reading programs are worthy goals; motivation and engagement can influence important short-term and long-term outcomes (e.g., enjoyment of reading, reading proficiency).

Supporting children's developing reading abilities involves more than properly executing one or more evidence-based reading programs. To be sure promising evidence-based instructional approaches and practices (e.g., systematic and explicit phonological awareness instruction, systematic and explicit phonics instruction, explicit and intentional vocabulary instruction) should be employed across classrooms.

It is imperative teachers root instruction in evidence-based practices and strive to make particularly good use of those shown to be most effective in high-quality empirical studies. However, evidence gathering should not be limited rigidly to culling outside information. The scholarly literature is a starting point; we begin inquiry into how best to support children's developing reading capabilities by evaluating and selecting programs and instructional approaches that best reflect what is known about how children learn to read. From this collection, we choose some approaches to try.

Inquiry does not end, however, once we have selected and employed one or more evidence-based programs for students. The interplay of the context and the unique makeup of each learner influences how well any evidence-based approach plays out on the ground. To be successful, educators must get to know and use what they learn from children, families, and the community to "co-construct learning inside the classroom and school" (Milner, 2021, p. 255).

For example, research suggests that young children just learning how to read should have ample opportunities to practice decoding words made up of the phonics patterns they have been taught directively. This is often accomplished by providing young readers with decodable texts—books that are almost entirely made up of words embodying the phonics patterns they have learned and are in the process of learning.

This practice of systematically teaching young children phonics patterns and then encouraging them to practice decoding words with those patterns is an evidence-based practice that should be employed regularly in classrooms to support students in developing beginning reading proficiency. However, matching decodable books to readers can be a significant challenge.

For example, some classrooms have a small collection of decodable texts, and the topics of the available books may prove uninteresting to the learner. The story lines of these books are also often quite simplistic to aid readability. Some children have minimal tolerance for such boredom. These issues, among others, can make students uninterested in the available books and, in turn, reluctant to read the decodable texts offered to them by adults.

Recall the case introduced in the preface of this text: Chrissy was largely disappointed by and disinterested in the books offered to her in her reading intervention. She identified the books as being a major factor in her not wanting to attend the intervention. Sure, Chrissy complied with the demands of the intervention. Many kids, like Chrissy, will do what they are asked to do by the teacher regardless of whether or not they enjoy and/or value school experiences. The power dynamic is clear; kids should do what they are asked by those who hold power over them or risk facing consequences.

Unfortunately, the educational system is not set up to encourage children to speak freely about whether they perceive lessons to be working for them. With an emphasis on compliance, students like Chrissy often quietly conform to methods that do not always support them. When children do resist, resistance is often not heard as self-advocating communication but dismissed as disobedience. However, as this book has emphasized, young children can share quite a bit about what they understand to be working and/or not working for them specific to school programs.

In many instances, we would be wise to listen carefully and respond thoughtfully to children's words, actions, and work. As noted in Chapter 4, teacher research affords us many approaches to listening that include but are not limited to interviewing children in participatory ways, conducting close observations of them at work, reviewing samples of their work, and simply encouraging informal feedback. It was during interviews that Chrissy shared various aspects of the evidenced-based reading intervention (e.g., books that did not match her interests, confusing letter tiles) that she perceived not to be working for her.

Oftentimes responding to children's insights does not require major changes to evidence-based programming. Making changes in response to children's and/or guardians' feedback can be as simple as it was in Chrissy's case: Chrissy's teacher simply swapped out one set of decodable texts for another and changed the form of letter manipulatives she was using. In other instances making changes can require a larger effort.

Classroom teachers and reading specialists often create their own sets of decodable texts to better engage students' individual interests and/or to help students see themselves in their reading experiences. We have observed educators work to gain students access to reading programs that would not have otherwise been available to them; we know teachers in districts with multiple elementary schools who have fought to allow children to participate in programs across schools. And we have witnessed, educators apply for and receive grants to update classroom libraries to better reflect the interests and cultures of students.

In each of these instances, educators were fighting for educational equity. They believed that their students not only had a right to learn to read but also had a right to learn in ways that were personally meaningful and engaging. Students in remedial reading interventions are already at a disadvantage compared to their typically achieving peers. Additionally, some are aware that they are not reading as well as peers and are uncomfortable being identified for extra support. Some struggle to find joy in reading. Some are concerned about what they miss when they leave the classroom/an activity to receive reading support.

When we make the decision to put aside these concerns because we believe (in alignment with strong evidence) that reading well enables one to live well, and so we require children who are not meeting benchmarks to enroll in additional programming to develop foundational reading skills, we must remember our responsibility to also support these children in actively engaging in the programming we are pushing. It makes good sense from an equity perspective to maximize children's investment in their reading interventions.

Children who engage willingly and eagerly in their lessons are more likely to reap the rewards of those lessons than if they avoided engagement and/or participated less actively or often. Therefore, children who are the furthest behind in developing reading proficiency deserve the most motivating and engaging opportunities to catch up. Striving readers should recognize time spent in reading interventions as time well spent; if they do not, one or more aspects of the program likely need to be adjusted.

The science of reading movement has shined a spotlight on what is known about how the brain learns to read and on a myriad of pedagogical approaches likely to assist children in learning to read. This is good news for all children, but it is especially good news for those who are currently struggling or will struggle learning to read. That stated, as we learn about normative development and ways of making meaning, we cannot lose sight of children as individuals and of the context(s) that compound learning to read.

Each child arrives at school with a unique identity and set of life experiences. It is naive and potentially unethical to assume that an evidence-based program will sufficiently meet the needs (reading related and otherwise) of all learners. In closing, we reaffirm that conducting case studies of students' motivation for reading programs is one way to better understand each child as an individual. Conducting case studies permits the teacher researcher to get to know students on a deeper level. Additionally, it sends the message to students that they and their perceptions of programming matter.

In putting the individual child and their needs and interests at the center, case studies can disrupt the traditional power structure found in many schools that functions effectively to minimize the amount of critical feedback students offer and maximize compliance within the status quo. Imagine the potential for advantageous outcomes if educators made good use of reading science while maximizing students' motivation and engagement within reading programs.

Amplifying students' voices and listening carefully to what they have to say within a case study approach to classroom research has the potential to improve reading programs grounded in the best reading science currently has to offer. By listening more, we can better relate reading instruction to children's own priorities and, in turn, improve their reading-related outcomes now and for years to come. When we ask children about their reading experiences, and listen, sincerely listen, to the reasons their voices express for wanting or not wanting to read, we can serve them and all learners better.

REFERENCES

Hatch, J. A. (2012). Introduction. In G. Perry, B. Henderson, & D. R. Meier, *Our inquiry, our practice: Undertaking, supporting, and learning from early childhood research(ers)* (pp. ix). NAEYC Books.

Milner, H. R. (2021). *Start where you are, but don't stay there: Understanding diversity, opportunity gaps, and teaching in today's classrooms* (2nd ed.). Harvard Education Press.

Index

advocacy, ix, 3, 105, 111, 118, 128
Algozzine, B., 43, 109
American Psychological Association (APA), 120
annual conferences, 110
APA. *See* American Psychological Association
Archambault, I., 27
artifacts, 40, 53; MMRP survey as, 46–48; student work as, 46, *46*, 52
assent, child, 20, 33, 49, 63

Bandura, A., 29
Berkeley Puppet Interview, 32
bias, 20–21, 45, 121

case study: boundaries and examples in, 15, *16*, *17*; case defining in, 15; Creswell and Poth on methodology of, 13–14; data analysis plan in, xxv; data use and collection for, xxv, 17–18, 58, 69–70; description and themes result in, 18–19; ethical manner research in, 19, 21; Excel use in, xxv; guide for, xxiv; inquiry question drafting in, 20–21; inquiry stance and, 118, 124; insights and innovations shaping in, xxiv; IRB and, 19; literature surveys and, 26; major advantage of, 13; methodology overview of, xxiv–xxv; MMRP as validated survey for, 14; motivation and multiple factors in, xvii–xviii; "object of study" focus in, 15; potential cases jot down for, 19; primary goal of, 4; program-specific information in, 14; project involvement as voluntary and confidential, 20; qualitative and quantitative data analysis for, xxv, xxviii; quantitative measure and qualitative methods combination in, 14; reading program, 130; real-life bounded system exploration in, 21; relevant literature synthesizing in, xxv; as research design, xvii; rights of parents and students in, 19–20, 21; sharing findings in, xxv–xxvi; soul-searching in, xxiv; student deep knowledge in, 19; three iterations inquiry exercise for, *22*; you and team function in, 15
children, 31; CRC and, ix, xi, xxiii, 2, 32; data analysis and collection involving, 40, 52, 81–82; educators and, ix, xi, xxiv; ideas and expertise model of, x; inquiry process involvement of, xvii,

120–21; interview methods for, 48; MMRP completing by, *47*; reading experiences of, ix, xi, xxiii, 1, 8; reading instruction and, 6; reading programs of, xxiii, 2, 4–5, 129; rights of, 2, 19–20, 21

children, eliciting perceptions of, xxiii, 2, 34; Clark and Moss Mosaic approach for, 33; common concerns in, 32

Church, M., xiv

Clark, A., 33, 50, 120

class or group level analysis: mean and median use in, 97; sample size and statistics in, 96–97; standard deviation in, 97–98

Cochran-Smith, M., 116–17

codes and coding, *80*, 82, *82*, *83*, 85

Cohen, D. H., 121

colleague communication, 107–8

Common Core State Standards, 3

Compton, D. L., 8–9

Condie, C., 31

consent, 20, 63

conversational drawing interview, 71–72, 120; clarifying questions use and examples for, 49–50; guardian or school counselor in, 60–61; walking-tour interviews and, 51–52

Cordray, D. S., 8–9

COVID-19 pandemic, xvi–xvii

CRC. *See* United Nations Convention on the Rights of the Child

Creswell, J. W., 13–14

Dana, N. F., 80–81, 84, 87, 111

data analysis, formative, 69–70, 73, 87; jottings and important project decisions in, 79–80; journal entries with descriptions in, *78*; major theme development in, 80

data analysis, summative, 69–73, 87; breaking up data in, 82; codes and early coding table in, 82, *82*; coding and memoing in, 80, 85; convergence and divergence points and patterns in, 85; description stage in, 80–81; discrepancy rectifying in, 85; end of study process of, 80; implications list in, 85–86; main points discussion in, 81; memo generation in, 83–84; observations and self-reports in, 84; peer review for, 84–85; quantitative data and, 68; research questions in, 80; revised coding table in, *83*; schooling in general points in, 86; sense making stage and practice exercise in, 81–84, *87–89*; summary of relevant scholarly literature review in, 81; teacher high priority actions in, 86; triangulation of findings in, 84; visual data patterns in, 84

data analysis plan, xxv; case study questions in, 70; data reviewing and refining in, 70–71; data source variety in, 70; exercise for, *74–75*; formative and summative analysis in, 70, 71, 72, 73; interviews and drawing and jottings reviews in, 71–72; journal entries and field notes insights in, 71; MMRP and, 71–72; observation commonalities or patterns in, 71; student documentation in, 72; walking tour jottings and interviews in, 72–73; "why" understanding in, 73

data collection: artifacts as, 40, 46–48; case studies and, xxv, 17–18, 58, 69–70; child and teacher and neutral observer views in, 52; children sharing understandings and opinions in, 40; daily diary entries review in, 17–18; data selection exercise for, *54*; evidence sources in, 40; imbalance of power mitigation for, 39; interviews as, 48–52; listening importance in, 39; multiple types and sources in, 17, 18; observations as, 41–46; participatory research methods in, 39–40; patterns and

discrepancies awareness in, 17; reading motivation pre- and post-measurement in, 18; student-led walking tours as, 40; triangulation use in, 40, 52, 53; trustworthiness of findings in, 40, 52, 53
data collection plan: case study questions for, 58, 70; co-teacher observations in, 61–62; daily morning schedule consideration in, 57–58; data collection plan exercise for, 65; data folders creation in, 63; data source specifications in, 58, 59; drawing interviews with guardian or school counselor in, 60–61; electronic filing system use in, 62–63; field notes template use in, 61; intentional planning for, 62; Izzy classroom research role and, 57; journal reflections use in, 59–60; master file creation in, 62–63; MMRP administration in, 60; multiple forms of data in, 64; saturation point in, 63–64; spreadsheet creation for, 63; triangulation process in, 58, 64; trustworthiness in, 64
data folders creation, 63
data source variety, 17, 18, 58, 59, 69, 70
Debey, E., 6
Deci, E., 29
decodable texts, 115–16, 128–29
Delpit, L., 106
diary, 17–19, 41, 52
Dogra, N., 120

Eccles, Jacquelynne, 29
Eckert, T. L., 5
educational equity, 117–18, 122–23, 129
educators, reading motivation of children and, ix, xi, xxiv
electronic filing system, 62–63
empowerment, xi, 105, 106

engagement: adults "know" misconception of, 7; reading program, xiv; SMILE acronym of, 30–31
Erickson, J. D., xi, xxvi, 16, 31; research of, ix–x
ethical and legal requirements, observations and, 45–46
ethical research, 19, 21
Excel, xxv, 92, 93, 94

field notes, 41, 42–43, 52–53, 61–62, 71
Fives, A., 5
Fuchs, D., 8–9
Fuchs, L. S., 8–9

Gambrell, L., 30, 34
Google Scholar, 35
Guthrie, J. T., 29, 33–34

Hancock, D. R., 43, 109
Harris, P., photo-sorting activity of, 33
Hatch, J. A., xiii

ILA. See International Literacy Association
inquiry question, drafting of: attempts at, 20; second and third follow-up questions for, 21; SEVT and, 20; three iterations inquiry question exercise for, 22
inquiry stance: access and equity and power issues in, 117, 122; behavior and self-reports in, 121; case study of students motivation major steps for, 118; child observation techniques in, 120–21; children involvement in, xvii; children's own insights in, 120; current research importance in, 119; engagement dimensions in, 121; equity issues and educational equity advancement in, 117–18; equity reflection questions for, 123; first project completion and, 117; five tips for taking, 119–23, 124; as habit of

mind, 117; Hope and decodable texts replacement in, 115; instructional planning exercise for, *124–26*; listen and observe students often in, 120; multiple perspectives and team use in, 121–22; Niko and sharing with friend in, 116; professional organizations and, 119–20; reflective journal and open-ended reflections for, 122; Reggio educators and, 119; regularly monitor students' motivation in, 117; research and teaching and activism in, 117–18; systematic inquiry and following up in, 116; teacher case study findings and changes in, 124; teacher researchers and multiple research projects in, 118; Trent and decodable dinosaur text creation in, 115–16

Institutional Review Board (IRB), 27; case study and, 19; presentation requirements of, 104

intentional planning, 62

International Literacy Association (ILA), 110, 119

interviews, 40, 53; conversational drawing in, 49–50; data analysis plan and, 71–73; description and themes regarding, 18, 19; methods for children, 48; observations compared to, 41; participatory, xv, 8; walking-tour in, 50–52

IRB. *See* Institutional Review Board

Jacobs, J. E., 27

jottings, 19, 57, 71–73, 79–80

journal entry: data analysis and collection plans in, 59–60, 71, *78*; inquiry stance reflections in, 122; observations use of, 41, *44–45*, 52

Journal of Practitioner Research, 111

Kuh, L. P., 62

Lewis, C.S., ix

listening, importance of, 39, 120, 128–30

Literacy Research Association (LRA), 110, 120

LRA. *See* Literacy Research Association

Lytle, S. L., 116–17

Malaguzzi, L., 119

Marinak, B., 30, 34, 92–93

Massachusetts Reading Association (MRA), 110

master file creation, 62–63

Mazzoni, S. A., 34

mean and median, use of, 97

Me and My Reading Profile (MMRP), 34, 63, 70–71; administration guidelines review for, 47; as case study survey, 14; child completing, *47*; class or group level analysis in, 96–98; data collection plan and, 60; data range in, 93, 95; Excel spreadsheet set-up in, 93, *94*; formative and summative analysis of, 68–69; general motivation change and, 47–48; "literacy out loud" construct in, 47; minimum and maximum response values for, 92; pre- and post- and overall scores in, 93; pre-formatted Excel template for, 93; quantitative analysis exercises for, *99–101*; random order in, 92; reader general self-concept measurement in, 47; as reading motivation survey artifact, 46–47; regular monitoring with, 91–92; results use of, 47; Rocky and, 91; scoring design of, 92–93; simple statistical analyses with, 92; student level analysis in, 95–96; three subscales of, 92–93; two levels of analysis in, 95; variably scaled items in, 92

Measelle, J. R., 6–7, 32

memoing, 80, 83–86

MMRP. *See Me and My Reading Profile*

Morgan, P. L., 8–9
Morrison, K., xiv
Mosaic approach, 33
Moss, P., 33, 50, 120
motivation, xvii–xviii, 26–28; data collection and plan in, 18, 58, 60; educators and, ix, xi, xxiv; inquiry stance and, 117–18; MMRP and, 46–48; in presentations, 105, 106; reading instruction regarding, 8–9; reading programs concerning, xiii, xiv, xvi, 3, 127; SMILE acronym and, 31
MRA. See Massachusetts Reading Association
Murphy, A., *xvii*
myths, reading instruction and, 5–6

National Council of Teachers of English (NCTE), 110, 120
National Reading Curriculum, 7
National Writing Project, 110
NCTE. See National Council of Teachers of English
Nixon, V., *xvii*
North Dakota Study Group, 110
"object of study," 15

observations, 40, 120–21; behavior identification in, 45; biases mitigation for, 45; careful review of, 52; clear pattern identification in, 41; co-teacher, 61–62; in data analysis, 71, 84; ethical and legal requirements following for, 45–46; field note excerpt sample for, *42–43*; field notes advantage in, 41, 52; five important guidelines for, 43, 45–46; interviews compared to, 41; principal and field notes in, 53; reflective diary or journal entries use in, 41, 52; reflective journal entry sample for, *44–45*; researchers' use of, 41; template creation for, 45; trust relationship development in, 45

Occasional Papers, 111
oral presentation, 110–11
O'Reilly, M., 120

participant identity protection, 104
participatory interviews, xv, 8
participatory research methods, 7, 39–40
peer review, 29, 84–85
PEN. See Progressive Education Network
personal blogs, 111
phonics instruction, xv, 59, 64, 128
PIGs. See Practitioner Inquiry Groups
PLCs. See Professional Learning Communities
Ponte, I. C., 62
Poth, C. N., 13–14
Practitioner Inquiry Groups (PIGs), 109
presentations: advocacy in, 105; annual conferences as, 110; case study write-up and presentation planning exercise for, *112–13*; clarify and refine for, 105; colleague communication and own projects in, 107–8; empowerment and sharing in, 105; inspire others with, 107–8; interactive experience for, 109; IRB requirements in, 104; oral presentation in, 110–11; organizations for, 110; outside of school community impact of, 107–8; participant identity protection in, 104; personal blogs and professional journals as, 111; PIGs sharing approach in, 109; PLCs and, 110; power structure and student representation in, 106–7; Prezi and Padlet use for, 109; reading motivation literature and SEVT familiarity in, 105; regular monitoring and student support in, 106; research report sections for, 108–9; research sharing and, 111–12; slideshow creation for, 109; "speed dating" activity for, 110; spelling

routine engagement and, 108; student achievement and empowerment in, 106; study findings and stakeholder sharing in, 104; teacher researchers and ripple effect of, 111; writing and, 111; writing your project in, 105
Prezi, 109
professional journals, 111
Professional Learning Communities (PLCs), 110
professional organizations, 119–20
Progressive Education Network (PEN), 110

qualitative data, analysis of, xxv, xxviii, 14, 73; commonalities and points of divergence in, 69–70; daily data review in, 69; formative and summative analysis and big picture in, 69
quantitative data, analysis of, 73; case study and, xxv, xxviii, 14; exercises for, *99–101*; inquiry focus decision in, 68; MMRP and formative and summative analysis in, 68–69; multiple data sources and, 69

reading experiences: children and early impact of, 1, 8; children as participants in, xi; children efficacious feelings in, xxiii; children's voices and, ix; educator and child empowerment in, xi; Fives and Eckert and Scanlon on, 5; positive, xxiii; Schiefele on reading involvement in, 4; school leaders and educators regarding, xxiv
reading intervention program(s). *See* reading program(s)
reading motivation surveys, 46–47
reading program(s): adjustments to practice and programming in, 2; case studies and, 130; children insights responding in, 129; children perception examination in, xxiii, 2; children's developing motivation within, 5; children's own views about, 4; children's rights in, xxiii; Chrissy case study in, xiv–xvi, 4, 8, 39, 128, 129; Daniel in, 13; decodable texts creation for, 129; dissatisfaction experience in, xvi; educational equity and, 129; engagement in, xiv; evidence-based instructional approaches and practices in, 127; go along to get along attitude in, xiv; grade-level reading benchmarks emphasis in, 5; Josh walking tour interview about, 25–26; motivation role in, xiv, xvi, 3, 127; opinions and ideas voicing encouragement in, 1; poor motivation in, xiii, xvi; power dynamic and compliance in, 128; racial and social and cultural disconnect in, xiii; reading motivation theorist and, 2; Sadie question about, 1; sharing findings in, 2; skills acquisition in, xxiii; student voices and listening importance in, 128–30; trustworthiness lack in, 6, 13
The Reading Teacher, 111
Reggio Emilia philosophy, 119
response to intervention (RTI), 5
Ritchhart, R., xiv
Rousseau, K., xxv, 57–64, 70–73
RTI. *See* response to intervention
Ryan, R., 29

Saint-Exupery, Antoine de, xi
saturation point, 63–64
Scanlon, D. M., 5
Schiefele, U., 4
scholarly research database, 28
school counselor, 60–61
self-efficacy, 29–30, 33, 124
self-reports, 84, 121
Situated Expectancy-Value Theory (SEVT), 9, 20, 67, 105, 115; "Can I do this?" part of, 3; cost and, 4;

"Do I want to do this, and why?" components of, 4, 25; as motivation theory, 3; pedagogical and content changes in, 4; reading motivation scholars and, 28; SMILE acronym alignment with, 29–31
skill acquisition, xxiii–xxiv, 3, 86, 105–7, 109
slideshow creation, 109
SMILE acronym, 33–34; engagement in, 30–31; importance in, 30; liking and intrinsic task enjoyment in, 30; meaningful choices in, 30; peer collaboration in, 29; reading motivation findings overview of, 31; self-efficacy in, 29–30; SEVT alignment in, 29–31; sharing in, 29; short-term and long-term goals in, 30; teacher connection in, 29
snowballing, 28, *34–35*, 46
soul-searching, xxiv, *10*
"speed dating" activity, 110
stakeholders, 2, 9, 104
stimulated recall procedure, 68
student level analysis: bar graph and, 96; difference score in, 95–96; graphic representation of differences in, *95*; subscale score examination in, 96; total score in, 95
Summer Institute on Descriptive Inquiry, 110
systematic inquiry and follow-up, 116

theme identification and patterns, 18–19, 41, 71, 84–85
trends, in reading motivation, 26, 27–28
triangulation, 40, 52, 53, 58, 64, 84
trustworthiness, 6, 13, 40, 52, 53, 64

United Nations Convention on the Rights of the Child (CRC), xxiii, 32; Article 12 of, ix, xi; children's rights in, 2

video recording, 57

walking-tour interviews, 120; conversational drawing interviews and, 51–52; data analysis plan and, 72–73; guardian or school counselor in, 61; other trusted adult use in, 50; space of interest tour questions for, 51; as student-led, 40, 50
Wharton-McDonald, R., 31
Wigfield, A., 27–28, 29, 33–34
Willingham, D. T., 8

Yendol-Hoppey, D., 80–81, 84, 87, 111
Young Children, Voice of Practitioners section of, 111

About the Author and Contributors

Joy Dangora Erickson, PhD, is an assistant professor of education in the School of Education at Endicott College. She received the Student Outstanding Research Award from the Literacy Research Association in 2018 for her work examining young children's motivation. In addition to exploring children's motivation to read within intervention programs, Erickson is interested in issues of early education for citizenship. Her work has been featured in numerous journals including: *The Reading Teacher*; *Literacy Research: Theory, Method, and Practice*; *Reading & Writing Quarterly: Overcoming Learning Difficulties*; *Journal of Early Childhood Literacy*; *Democracy & Education;* and *Journal of Curriculum Studies*.

Carla M. Evans, PhD, is a senior associate at the National Center for the Improvement of Educational Assessment (Center for Assessment). She is actively engaged with projects that attempt to bridge the gap between classroom assessment and large-scale assessment. Evans supports states in designing and implementing innovative assessment and accountability reforms, especially those that rely on performance assessments. She is also working in multiple states to support the design and implementation of balanced assessment systems with a particular focus on scaling and sustaining assessment literacy initiatives with K–12 teachers and school/district leaders. Evans's's research focuses on the impacts and implementation of assessment and accountability policies on teaching and learning.

Beth Fornauf, PhD, is a research associate at the Center for Applied Special Technology (CAST). Her research examines Universal Design for Learning (UDL) and disability studies as complementary frameworks for inclusive, equity-oriented pedagogy in K–12 and teacher education. She collaborates with school districts across New England to support applications of UDL, as well as the recruitment, preparation, and retention of equity-oriented, inclusive special education teachers. In addition to her role at CAST, Fornauf teaches courses in disability studies and special education at Plymouth State University and the Harvard Graduate School of Education.

Cara E. Furman, PhD, is an associate professor of literacy education at the University of Maine at Farmington. She is coauthor of *Descriptive Inquiry in Teacher Practice: Cultivating Practical Wisdom to Create Democratic Schools* and publishes in journals such as *Curriculum Inquiry, Education and Culture, Studies in Philosophy and Education*, and *Teachers College Record*. Furman researches teacher development as it intersects with inquiry, assets-based inclusive teaching, and progressive literacy practices.

Luke Reynolds, PhD, taught middle and secondary English in public schools for many years before becoming an associate professor of education at Endicott College. The father of four sons, Reynolds is also the author of *Surviving Middle School: A Call to Creativity* and many books for teachers and kids.

Kyleigh P. Rousseau is a kindergarten classroom teacher who lives in New England with her husband and rescue dog. Her passion for early childhood education began in 2010 at the University of New Hampshire, where she received both a bachelor of science degree and a master's of education. Rousseau has experience teaching early childhood education internationally and domestically in the United States.

Alessandra E. Ward, EdD, is an assistant professor of education at Wheaton College in Massachusetts, where she teaches courses in early childhood and elementary literacy methods and social and emotional learning, and supervises the senior practicum. She is interested in the literacy engagement of primary grade learners, particularly in contexts that prioritize culturally responsive pedagogy. She is also an interdisciplinary curriculum writer for Great First Eight, an assets-based, all-day curriculum that centers on equity and justice for 0–8-year-old children living and learning in metropolitan areas. Ward's work has been published in *The Reading Teacher; Journal of Adolescent and Adult Literacy; Literacy Research: Theory, Method, and Practice; Literacy Now;* and *Language Arts*.

Ruth Wharton-McDonald, PhD, is an associate professor of education at the University of New Hampshire (UNH), where she teaches courses in literacy, children's literature, and a doctoral proseminar. Her interest in children's literacy and teacher preparation stems from her experiences as a classroom teacher, a reading specialist, a school psychologist, and a supervisor of elementary teaching interns. Wharton-McDonald spends as much time as she can in classrooms talking with children, and for the past decade, she has directed Seacoast Reads, a volunteer mentoring/literacy support program pairing UNH undergraduates and children in local schools, libraries, and after school programs.

www.ingramcontent.com/pod-product-compliance
Lightning Source LLC
Chambersburg PA
CBHW030140240426
43672CB00005B/198